"As the Legendary Voice of I
hundreds of thousands of
world. Jason's challenging j..a exemplifies
everything IRONMAN stands for: the refusal to quit, the courage
to start when success seems impossible, and the transformation that
happens when ordinary people attempt extraordinary things. This is a
story that needed to be told."

—**MIKE REILLY**, the Voice of IRONMAN

"Jason doesn't give you a cute comeback story, he gives you truth, pain,
setbacks, surgeries, doubt, and the grit to keep showing up anyway. *From
37 Yards to Kona* is proof that ordinary people can do outrageous things
when they stop whining and start working. Read this, then go earn your
finish line."

—**JAMES LAWRENCE**, "The Iron Cowboy,"
two-time Guinness World Record holder, author, and speaker

"Jason's journey—from barely managing a single swim lap to standing on
the starting line of the IRONMAN World Championship—is a powerful
testament to what becomes possible when unwavering determination
meets intentional preparation. This book is a blueprint for anyone who has
ever questioned their own potential, and Jason's story invites each of us to
consider what transformation might look like in our own lives."

—**MEREDITH KESSLER**, professional triathlete, 11-time IRONMAN
champion, 20-time IRONMAN 70.3 champion, and author

"If you value authenticity as much as I do, you will love reading Jason's
story of transformation. His transparent reflections on faith and fitness
offer insights not just for athletes, but for anyone pursuing turning dreams
into realities or grappling with healthy direction amid life's challenges. You
will be inspired by the intersecting themes of trust, discipline, purpose,
endurance, balance, resilience, and relationships that affirm we are never

alone in our journey. As a fellow pastor, IRONMAN triathlete, and coach, I am honored and blessed to be part of Jason's amazing story."

—**COACH SCOTT BENNEFIELD**, nine-time IRONMAN finisher
and founder of Para Endurance

"*From 37 Yards to Kona* is a gripping story of perseverance and the deep difference between doing and becoming. The moment Jason describes dragging himself those first 37 yards offers a vulnerable picture of how God begins His greatest work in our smallest, most humbling beginnings. This book reminds us that endurance sports can be a sacred classroom, shaping our faith as much as our fitness. Athletes and ministry leaders will find strong encouragement here— especially those who see sport not just as competition but as transformation, personal growth, and a platform to point others to Christ."

—**MARK LONG**, director, FCA Endurance

"I've known Jason Millsaps for over 20 years and have had the privilege of witnessing his remarkable journey firsthand. He stands as a living example of what can happen when someone decides, "I want to change." This isn't the story of a superathlete endowed with rare talent; it's the story of an ordinary man who met life's challenges with determination, humility, and unwavering consistency, proving that extraordinary results are born from ordinary perseverance. If you're seeking inspiration to live beyond the ordinary, this book will both challenge and encourage you to do just that."

—**DR. BJ DAVIS**, music director and film composer

"I still remember the phone call I received from Jason. He said, "Hey, man, what would you think about running a 5K?" I had no idea my response to that question would lead to significant changes in my life. Because I said yes, my wife and I are able to enjoy daily exercise. Jason's encouragement changed my life."

—**KEVIN LINTHICUM**, Pastor of Discipleship, Senior Adults,
Missions, Southmont Baptist Church, Denton, TX

"This man isn't quitting!" That was my first note on Jason Millsaps, and first impressions are often spot on. The journey to becoming an IRONMAN finisher is a metaphor for both faith and life, a pursuit that strips away pretense and forces you to confront the raw edges of human potential. *From 37 Yards to Kona* is Jason's powerful testimony, a stark reminder that the most formidable barrier between you and your aspirations is often not lack of physical strength, but the pervasive grip of fear.

Jason's honest reflection on silencing doubt and taking that crucial first step (signing up for a one-month swim pass) provides an essential lesson for anyone paralyzed by the scale of their dreams. Going from not finishing one lap to tackling a 2.4-mile swim, 112-mile bike, and 26.2-mile run requires more than guts; it demands unwavering commitment to a seemingly unreachable vision. Jason's journey reminded me that when your foundation is faith (in God and yourself), nothing is impossible. His testimony resonates because it speaks to the resilience required when the body screams to stop but the spirit urges continuation.

From 37 Yards to Kona challenges us to shed fear, embrace growth's pain, and harness community strength. I am inspired by him, proud to know him, and honored to call him my friend. Pick up his book and let his remarkable testimony ignite the fire within you to pursue your own extraordinary finish line."

—COACH ELIZABETH INPYN, founder of INPYN
and former NCAA Division I athlete

"Inspirational! Jason Millsaps's heroic triathlon journey is a story of courage, discipline, perseverance, faith, and family. It is a road map for anyone seeking a healthier and more productive life. Read this book and become a better person."

—COL. (RET.) ROLAND J. TISO JR., US Army, author of *In Strange Company: An American Soldier with Multinational Forces in the Middle East and Iraq*

FROM
37 YARDS
TO KONA

Published by Jason Millsaps, Tampa, Florida

Cover design and author photo by Patrick Clark

ISBN: 979-8-9939060-0-3

Printed in the United States of America

First Edition: 2026

www.121TriCoaching.com

FROM
37 YARDS
TO KONA

HOW THE WORST SWIM OF MY LIFE
LED TO TRIATHLON'S BIGGEST STAGE

JASON MILLSAPS

FOREWORD BY LANCE WITT

MEDICAL AND TRAINING DISCLAIMER

This book chronicles the author's personal journey through endurance athletics and medical recovery. It is not intended as medical advice, training prescription, or nutrition guidance for any individual reader.

CONSULT PROFESSIONALS BEFORE:

- Beginning any new exercise program
- Making significant dietary changes
- Attempting endurance events
- Ignoring pain or injury symptoms
- Making decisions about medical treatment

THE AUTHOR'S EXPERIENCES INCLUDE:

- Racing with undisclosed injuries (not recommended)
- Two spinal surgeries with extended recovery periods
- Personal nutrition strategies developed with professional guidance
- Training protocols designed by certified coaches
- What worked for the author may not be appropriate, safe, or effective for every individual. Age, fitness level, medical history, and current health status all impact what training is appropriate for you.

MEDICAL PROCEDURES DESCRIBED:

The surgical procedures and recovery protocols described in this book reflect the author's specific medical situation under the care of licensed physicians. These descriptions are for informational purposes only and should never replace consultation with your own qualified health-care providers.

TRAINING ADVICE:

While the author is a certified triathlon coach (USAT Level 1, Training-Peaks Level 2), the training experiences shared in this book are personal narrative, not individualized coaching. Readers interested in structured training should work with certified coaches who can assess their specific needs, abilities, and limitations.

LIABILITY DISCLAIMER:

CONTENTS

DEDICATION

To Andrea,

You are the unsung hero of every finish line I've crossed, believing in me even when I didn't believe in myself. Those 4 a.m. alarms weren't about me choosing the bike; they were about making room for everything that mattered. I trained in the dark so I could be fully present for you, our boys' games and band concerts, and all the other moments that make up a life together. You made sure our family never took a back seat, and I am grateful you held me to that standard.

Every six-hour training ride meant you carried extra weight at home, and you never complained. Every race weekend became a "race-cation" that we turned into adventures together. You celebrated my victories and carried me through my defeats. You stood by me through two back surgeries, countless setbacks, and the stubborn pursuit of a dream that could have pulled us apart, but instead, you helped me weave it into the fabric of our family.

This book, and every race it chronicles, belongs to you as much as it does to me. Your strength, patience, and unwavering support made all of it possible. I couldn't have finished a single mile without you. We are a team and will always be one.

I love you more than words can express.

To Jonathan and Jaden,

You grew up watching your dad chase something that seemed crazy at times. You spent countless weekends tracking me on race apps, standing in the heat waiting for me to run past. Thank you for your patience and for the times you said "Good job, Dad" even when you were bored watching me run in circles.

I hope that watching this journey taught you something valuable: that ordinary people can accomplish extraordinary things when they refuse to quit, that setbacks don't have to be endings, and that discipline and faith can carry you through anything. But more than any race or medal, I hope you know this: You two are my greatest accomplishments. No finish line will ever matter more than being your dad. I am proud of you both. I love you both.

Always.

ACKNOWLEDGMENTS

This book represents 12 years of chasing a dream, but I never ran alone.

Coach Scott Bennefield, you saw potential in me over a salad bar when I could barely swim two laps. You didn't just coach me through training plans, you believed in me before I believed in myself. Your patience, wisdom, and steady encouragement carried me through countless moments of doubt. Eight IRONMAN races seemed impossible until I met someone who had done it and was willing to show me the way. Thank you for being that person. Your friendship and mentorship changed my life.

Coach Elizabeth Inpyn, you transformed how I understand nutrition and fueling. What started as learning to eat properly for race day became a wealth of knowledge I now share with my own coaching clients. Your expertise helped me not only race better but live healthier. Thank you for your patience with my questions and for teaching me that proper nutrition isn't restriction, it's strategic fueling for performance. You taught me to view food as an ally in training, not an obstacle to manage. That mindset shift was as important as any workout.

Mom and Dad, you've supported every crazy pursuit I've ever attempted. From driving me to soccer practices and piano lessons as a kid to teaching me the work ethic that made 13-month training cycles possible, to flying across the country approximately one million times to watch your grandsons so Andrea and I could race together, you've always been there.

Mom, I'm sorry for taking years off your life every time you checked the race tracker and saw I was "behind pace" on the bike. I know you were convinced I had either crashed into a ditch or gotten lost due to my lack of any sense of direction. For the record: I was fine, just slow. Dad, thanks for keeping Mom from calling race officials to send out a search party.

You both taught me to finish what I start, to work hard, and to pursue excellence. This book exists because of the foundation you built and because you were willing to become full-time grandparent-babysitters so your son could swim, bike, and run in circles for 140.6 miles. I promise the investment paid off. Eventually.

My church family at Bell Shoals, thank you for supporting a worship pastor who occasionally showed up on Monday mornings barely able to walk after weekend races. Your encouragement, prayers, and understanding when I needed flexibility for race travel meant more than you know. You've cheered me on from Florida while I raced in different places, and you celebrated each finish like it was your own.

Kevin, my running partner through those painful Couch to 5K mornings, you showed up at 4 a.m. when we could barely run 60 seconds. Thanks for suffering through those early miles with me. Thanks for always being an encouragement to me. Thanks for being a true friend.

Dr. Michael Fromke, thank you for your expertise, patience, and care throughout this journey. I'm grateful for the time you took to walk me through every detail, explaining my options, setting realistic expectations for recovery, and ensuring I understood each step of the process. Most importantly, thank you for the skill and precision you brought to the operating room. The screws and rods you placed didn't just fix my back, they gave me my life back, and they held up in those last races! Because of your work, I've been able to continue pursuing and achieving my goals. I couldn't have asked for a better surgeon.

To the countless volunteers, aid station workers, and spectators at every race—you'll never know how much your cheers mattered at mile 20 of the marathon when everything hurt. Thank you.

And to everyone who followed my journey on social media, sent encouraging messages, or prayed for me during races—thank you. Knowing people were tracking my progress and believing in me made the hard miles easier.

This journey taught me that remarkable accomplishments require everyday people to show up consistently, and that it helps tremendously to have the support of incredible communities. I'm grateful to every person who played a part in mine.

FOREWORD

I got to know Jason Millsaps in 2018 when he reached out for some life coaching. When you meet Jason, he is very unassuming and unpretentious. But don't let that modest persona fool you. He comes across as an ordinary guy, but he possesses an extraordinary tenacity that just won't quit. Inside, deep in his core, he has a fire burning and an unrelenting will that drives him.

When Jason first decided to get in shape and change his physical condition, he could run for only 60 seconds at a time and could swim only 37 yards. From that inauspicious beginning, Jason would ultimately complete 16 IRONMAN competitions. This inspiring book chronicles Jason's journey each step of the way.

What you will discover in the pages that follow is that this book is not just about Jason's amazing physical accomplishments. It is really the story of a man who was internally transformed by the entire process. The rigorous training and meticulous preparation and debilitating setbacks and courageous perseverance became Jason's teacher. His identity, faith, marriage, and leadership were all strengthened and galvanized along the way. The person that Jason has become in the process really is the major headline of this book.

This entire book is laced with valuable life lessons and pearls of wisdom that can help you in the pursuit of your dreams. Even if you don't consider yourself an athlete or don't own a pair of running shorts, this book is still for you.

Like me, I believe you will find yourself inspired and motivated by Jason's story. Most of us will never compete in an IRONMAN, but we all have dreams and hopes and goals that we hold. As I read this book, I found myself asking, "What dream have I laid down? What goal have I given up on?" Maybe you need to ponder those questions as well.

The truth is, we are all in a race . . . a race called life. Your race is not Jason's race. As he says in the book,

The race is not against anyone else. It is against the voice that says you can't. Against the fear that says you are not enough. Against the past that says you already failed. The race is between who you are and who you could become.

The question is, Will you get started, and will you keep showing up?

I am excited for you to turn the page and hear the story of a man who refused to stop at 37 yards.

—Lance Witt
Life coach and creator of the One Life Process

AUTHOR'S NOTE

This book is about endurance, faith, and the stubborn refusal to quit. But before we begin, I want you to know a few things.

First, I'm a worship pastor and a man of faith, unashamed of my love for Jesus and the calling He has placed on my life. My relationship with God has been central to this journey, and I won't hide that. But if you don't share my faith or maybe you're not sure what you believe, I invite you to keep reading. The stuff about pushing through when you want to quit works for anybody.

Second, I'm a husband to an incredible wife, Andrea, and father to two sons who have watched this journey unfold since they were small. Much of what drove me wasn't just personal achievement; it was the desire to leave them a legacy. I wanted them to see that their dad didn't give up when things got hard. That faith matters. That persistence pays off. If this book serves no other purpose than to show my family what's possible when you refuse to quit, it will have been worth writing.

Third, this book chronicles my journey honestly, including decisions that were both inspiring and instructive, sometimes as cautionary tales. I raced with serious back injuries that eventually required two surgeries. I pushed through pain that probably warranted earlier intervention. My story shows both the power of persistence and the danger of ignoring your body's warnings. Please hear this clearly: There's a difference between productive discomfort that builds strength and destructive pain that causes lasting damage. Work with medical professionals. Listen to your body. Know when to push and when to rest. My experience taught me that sometimes the bravest thing isn't pushing through, it's choosing to heal properly.

Fourth, this isn't just a book for athletes. Your 140.6 might not involve swimming, biking, or running at all. It might be rebuilding after divorce, starting a business, recovering from illness, breaking an addiction, restoring a broken relationship, or simply showing up for your life when quitting feels easier. The distance doesn't matter. What matters is that you keep moving toward your finish line, even when the path is longer and harder than you imagined.

Finally, this book is as much about ordinary as it is about extraordinary. I'm not a professional athlete. I'm not naturally gifted at endurance sports. I'm a guy who refused to quit, who learned that persistence matters more than talent, and who knows that faith carries you when strength runs out.

Your race is waiting. Let's begin.

—Jason Millsaps

PART I

THE STARTING LINE

1

60 Seconds at a Time

*"The difference between the impossible
and the possible lies in determination."*
—**TOMMY LASORDA**

The Chinese philosopher Lao Tzu said, "A journey of a thousand miles begins with one step." In a way, my own journey began not with a literal step, but with a downloadable PDF of the Couch to 5K program.

Early 2010. I was still downing Red Bull and Diet Coke daily, still answering the 3 p.m. headaches with two Excedrin, still living the life of an out-of-shape worship pastor who spent more time in front of screens than taking care of his body. But something inside me was restless. I wanted to see if I could do something physical, something that required more than just showing up.

I didn't believe the Couch to 5K program would actually work, but I downloaded it anyway. The program promised to turn anyone, even an average person like me, into someone who could run 3.1 miles without stopping. I teamed up with one of my great friends, Kevin, and we agreed to meet early in the mornings to suffer through this together.

Those first sessions were humbling. Run for 60 seconds, then walk for 90. Repeat that until we either finished or died. Spoiler alert: Neither of us died, but some days it felt close. Running was no joke.

Week by week, 60 seconds became 90 seconds became two minutes. Our bodies were adapting, learning what muscles are supposed to do when you actually use them. We completed the program and could finally run a couple of miles without stopping, something that seemed impossible when we started.

Race day arrived for a local 5K, bringing with it the kind of nerves usually reserved for job interviews or first dates. At the starting line, I looked around and saw people who looked like real runners. They had the right shoes, the right gear, the right stride. I had a cotton T-shirt and a lot of doubt, wondering if we would survive what felt like the world's longest 5K.

We both finished the race. It wasn't fast or pretty, but we crossed the finish line. And that feeling, crossing a finish line you weren't sure you would reach, is unforgettable. I was hooked. None of my childhood participation trophies or medals compared to this feeling. This was earned. I know some of you are thinking, *It was just a 5K. Calm down.* But that 5K was a big deal for me at the time, a massive personal victory. That medal went straight to the corner of my dresser mirror, a daily reminder that effort creates transformation. I ran a couple more 5Ks and eventually completed a 10K. But I began to wonder: *What is my limit?*

The Ultimate Test

Soon after, I set my sights on the ultimate test, a full marathon. Twenty-six point two miles of possibility and pain.

Living in Albuquerque at 5,300 feet in elevation, I chose the Rock 'n' Roll San Diego Marathon in June 2010. Our boys were young—Jonathan was four and Jaden was only 16 months old—so Andrea and I turned the trip into a summer vacation. I would run the marathon at the beginning of our vacation, and then we would all head to Disneyland. Perfect plan.

I also thought that training at high altitude would give me an edge at sea level in San Diego, which sounded scientific enough to be true. I found a marathon training plan online that looked simple: Gradually increase your weekly mileage, do one long run per week, cross-train, rest. Easy enough.

Except I didn't really follow it.

Some runs I didn't complete. Some I didn't even start. My eating habits didn't change; I was still living on whatever was convenient, still downing energy drinks and sodas. My work habits didn't change either, still grinding late into the night, still chasing that 3 p.m. Excedrin.

But I would run the shorter distances, so a marathon couldn't be that much harder, right? I planned to just figure it out on race day. I know you're probably thinking, *This is a terrible plan*. Well, you would be right, but be patient with me. Sometimes I have to learn the hard way.

Race Day

Race morning arrived with perfect Southern California weather, cool, clear, coastal. I stood at the biggest starting line I had ever seen. There were 30,000 runners all sorted by their expected paces. So, of course, I confidently lined up with the nine-minute-per-mile group. Clearly an optimist.

The starting horn sounded, and the massive crowd surged forward like a slow-moving river. I settled into what felt like a comfortable pace, passing people, feeling strong. The energy was awesome, crowds cheering, and there were bands playing at every mile.

The first few miles ran on pure adrenaline. This was easier than I had expected. Why did people make such a big deal about marathons? Around mile 13, I checked my watch. Halfway done, and I was still feeling good. At this pace, I would certainly finish in under four hours, which sounded impressive. I had no idea if it was realistic for someone with my training, or lack thereof, but I wanted it.

"Fake it till you make it," right? That's what everyone says.

Turns out, you really can't fake preparation.

Mile 15. My quads started feeling tight. Nothing serious, just some fatigue setting in; I would push through. Mile 17. Both legs were hurting now. Not just tired, actual pain. Sharp, burning sensations shooting through my muscles with every stride. I slowed from a run to a shuffle, trying to shake it off. Mile 18. That's when I felt something I had never experienced before.

Suddenly, and I'm serious about this, both legs felt like they were broken. Not sore. Not cramping. Broken. I was convinced every bone in both legs had cracked or, worse, shattered. The pain was unlike anything I had ever felt. I stopped running entirely and hobbled to the side of the road, watching other runners stream past me.

A barefoot runner floated by like some minimalist, his feet barely touching the pavement. Meanwhile, I could barely lift my feet at all. I stood there trying to stretch, trying to shake out my legs, trying to understand what was happening. This wasn't normal fatigue. This was complete failure. My body was shutting down, rebelling against the abuse I had put it through by showing up unprepared. I started walking. Limping, really.

Around me, runners who had paced themselves properly were still moving with steady control. They knew something I didn't: that a marathon isn't won in the first half. It's survived in the second half through preparation and discipline. I really didn't know how everyone else still seemed to be moving so effortlessly.

All the training runs I had skipped were coming back to haunt me. Every shortcut I had taken, every "rest day" I'd actually needed but ignored, every long run I'd convinced myself wasn't necessary—they all mattered. And now I was paying the price.

I genuinely thought I would never walk normally again. I wasn't being dramatic; I was legitimately concerned that I had caused permanent damage to my legs. Miles 20 through 26 exist in my memory as a blur of pain, shame, and stubbornness. I walked most of it. Occasionally I would attempt a slow jog, but within seconds my legs would seize and force me back to walking. Other runners passed me in steady streams, people who looked fresh, people who were actually running, people who clearly understood something about training that I had completely missed.

Around mile 24, an older woman, probably in her 60s, jogged past me with perfect form and called out, "Looking good! Almost there!" I was not looking good. I was limping, had a grimace on my face, and was probably scaring spectators. But her encouragement gave me just enough energy to start shuffle-running again.

Mile 26. I could see the finish line in the distance. I could hear the music and hear the crowd cheering. I forced my broken legs into something resembling a run and crossed the finish line. Official time: I don't even remember. It seemed like a couple of days. I received my medal, but I was more concerned about how I would ever walk normally again.

When I finally limped back to find Andrea and the boys, she took one look at me. I could see both pride and concern on her face.

"You finished," she said, smiling carefully.

"Barely."

Jonathan looked up at me with wide eyes. "Daddy, can we go to Disneyland now?"

I looked down at my four-year-old son, then at Andrea holding Jaden, then at my legs that no longer functioned like legs should.

"I will never do that again," I said.

Andrea laughed softly. "You say that now."

"I'm serious. Never. That was the dumbest thing I've ever done."

She didn't argue. She just helped me limp to the car.

Disneyland on Broken Legs

The next few days were excruciating. Walking down stairs required holding the railing and descending one painful step at a time. Sitting down and standing up required strategy, planning, and sometimes Andrea's assistance. My legs were so sore that every movement hurt.

But worse than the physical pain was the knowledge that I had done this to myself. I had signed up and paid for something I didn't understand. I'd ignored the training plan. I'd assumed I could fake my way through with willpower alone. I still don't know how I managed to walk around Disneyland afterward. I have photos of me pushing the stroller with the boys, smiling for the camera, pretending everything was fine. But I remember the pain with every single step.

That medal, the one I nearly destroyed my body to earn, didn't feel like an achievement. It felt like evidence of poor judgment. When we got back to Albuquerque, I hung it up on the corner of our dresser, but I tried to pretend the whole thing had never happened.

The Seed

But here's what I didn't understand yet: That marathon taught me something I would spend the next two years trying to forget. Attempting big things without proper preparation doesn't make you brave. It makes you reckless. And recklessness doesn't end well.

Looking back now, I knew nothing, nothing about nutrition, pacing, training methodology, or the mental game of endurance. I was like someone who had watched a few YouTube videos about flying and then tried to pilot a plane. The confidence far exceeded the competence. That marathon represented something that most of us experience at some time or other: Try something hard. Do it halfway. Fail. Move on. Pretend it never happened. So I went back to what I knew: ministry work, late nights in the office, and the chemical cocktail of Red Bull, Diet Coke, and Excedrin that kept me functioning. The disappointment of that finish line faded into the background of a busy life. What I didn't know, what I couldn't see yet, was that sometimes you need to fail spectacularly before you're ready to succeed. Sometimes you need to crash and burn before you're willing to actually do the work.

The Real Beginning

The marathon broke me. But it also planted a seed. That seed would lie dormant for two years, buried under energy drinks and late nights and the slow drift back into unhealthy patterns. But in late July 2012, sitting in my home office at midnight, editing a church video, I would finally see clearly what I had become. And this time, when I decided to change, I wouldn't do it alone. I wouldn't do it halfway. And I wouldn't quit when it got hard. But first, I had to hit rock bottom.

As I stood at that finish line in San Diego, medal around my neck and legs barely functioning, I had no idea that this failure was actually the beginning of something much bigger. John C. Maxwell reminds us, "Everything worthwhile is uphill" (*The 15 Invaluable Laws of Growth*, 2012), and Kouzes and Posner affirm that leadership is forged in the crucible of challenge and perseverance (*The Leadership Challenge*, 2017).

The marathon taught me what doesn't work: shortcuts, arrogance, and lack of preparation. What I learned two years later was what does work: discipline, humility, and the willingness to be taught. But that lesson was still 26 months away.

2

The Wake-Up Call

"Only those who risk going too far can possibly find out how far one can go."
—T. S. ELIOT

For a worship pastor, late nights weren't unusual, planning worship services, editing videos, responding to emails. But tonight was different.

Late July 2012. Two years after the San Diego Marathon disaster. It was past midnight in Albuquerque when I saw him. I was staring at my computer in our guest bedroom that we'd turned into an office, editing yet another church announcement video. This was my routine: work all day planning worship services and leading ministry teams, come home for dinner, then head to the home office to grind on administrative tasks until my eyes burned. Andrea and the boys had been asleep for hours.

As I scrubbed through the footage, adjusting audio levels and cutting transitions, I caught a glimpse of the man on-screen making the announcements. He looked tired. Heavy. Worn down. It took me a moment to realize I was looking at myself. I know that sounds weird, but I hit pause and stared. When had I become this person? My face looked puffy, which is a nice way to say I had gained weight and looked unhealthy. But it was my eyes that stopped me. They looked empty, like someone going through the motions of living but not actually alive.

How had I not seen this before? How had I become so disconnected from the person staring back at me? I remember looking around the desk at the evidence of who I had become. My desk at the office was identical: a Red Bull and a bottle of Excedrin, the extra-strength kind that was the only thing that worked with my headaches. The mini-fridge in my office was full of Diet Coke with lime, and I knew there were at least four more Red Bulls chilling in there waiting for me to consume.

Every single day around 3 p.m., a crushing headache would hit. Every day, I would reach for two Excedrin and pray it would kick in fast enough to let me function. Every day, I would tell myself tomorrow would be different. Tomorrow never was.

I looked back at the frozen image on my screen. I wasn't lazy, I worked really hard, but this wasn't the man Andrea had married. This wasn't the father my boys deserved. This wasn't even close to the person I thought I was. But here's the thing about wake-up calls: They don't come with instruction manuals. They show you the truth and leave you to figure out what to do with it.

This wasn't the first time I had tried to change. Two years earlier, I had run a marathon, or, should I say, completed a marathon. I had convinced myself that crossing that finish line would transform me, that the medal would somehow make me into the person I wanted to be. It didn't.

I went right back to Red Bulls and late nights. The weight returned, plus some extra. The headaches came back worse than before. And that marathon medal now sat in a drawer somewhere, a reminder that trying hard without changing the underlying habits doesn't actually change anything.

The marathon had failed because I had treated it like an event to survive instead of a lifestyle to build. I had pushed my way through minimal training, destroyed my body on race day, and immediately returned to the behaviors that had made me unhealthy in the first place.

Sitting there at midnight, staring at that exhausted face on the screen, I realized the problem wasn't that I'd failed to finish the marathon, because I had finished it. The problem was that finishing hadn't changed me. I had collected the medal, and maybe this sounds too extreme, but I had gone right back to the life that was slowly killing me. A finish line without transformation is just a moment. And moments fade.

I turned off the computer and sat in the dark, and a question formed that would change everything: *If I don't change now, what will I look like in 5 years? And maybe worse, 10 years?* The answer wasn't good.

At this rate, I would be the pastor who died young from a heart attack or stroke. The dad who couldn't play with his kids because he was always tired. The husband who was physically present but emotionally absent, buried in work and sustained by energy drinks.

I thought about Jonathan, now almost seven years old, and Jaden, three and a half. What kind of example was I setting? That success means sacrificing your health? That leadership means running yourself into the ground? I thought about Andrea, who had watched me put myself through that marathon disaster, nursed me back to health, and then silently witnessed my slow return to the habits that had made the marathon necessary in the first place. She'd never said, "I told you so." However, she did lecture me about the energy drinks and late nights. I just didn't listen at first. Obviously, she was worried about me. And rightly so.

The Moment

We all have moments when life forces us to see ourselves clearly. Maybe it's stepping on a scale, looking at a credit card statement, or hearing your child repeat something you said in anger. Maybe it's sitting in a doctor's office getting news you weren't expecting, or realizing you can't remember the last time you laughed with your spouse. These moments can feel like endings, but they're actually beginnings. Mine began with a man on a screen who looked like he had given up. The problem was, that man was me.

But what I didn't know that night, sitting surrounded by the mess of my habits, was that this moment of seeing clearly would eventually lead me to swim 2.4 miles, bike 112 miles, and run 26.2 miles in a single day. Multiple times. Including at the World Championship in Kona, Hawaii. I couldn't have imagined that the guy who could barely recognize himself would one day stand at starting lines with some of the world's most elite athletes. But that's getting ahead of the story. First came the question that changed everything: *What if I actually tried to change? Not tomorrow. Not Monday. Not next month when things slow down. What if I started right now?*

The next morning, I woke up with the same pounding headache that had become my 3 p.m. partner. But instead of immediately reaching for the Excedrin, I lay there and thought about the man on the screen.

Andrea was already up, getting our oldest son ready for school while our youngest was making noise and a mess. I could hear their voices in the kitchen. This was the normal morning chaos that I usually tuned out while planning my day. But this morning, something was different. This morning, I was paying attention.

I walked into the kitchen and watched Andrea pack Jonathan's lunch while simultaneously trying to entertain Jaden. There were, of course, several reminders to Jonathan to brush his teeth. She moved like a pro every morning. There was never any downtime with two young boys in the house. Even though I had always provided for my family financially by working hard, was I missing something and truly just being a spectator in my own family?

"You okay?" Andrea asked. She always knows when something is weighing on me.

"I need to change some things," I said.

She paused, looking at me carefully. "Like what?"

I showed her the screenshot of the video I was working on, the frozen frame of the man who looked defeated. "All of it. The late nights. The headaches. The way I eat. The way I feel."

She didn't say anything immediately, but I know she was thinking she had already said these things to me. I know she was worried about my headaches. At one point she was convinced I had a brain tumor. She had already suggested I try going without the energy drinks to see if that helped with my headaches.

The First Challenge

I knew I needed to start somewhere. So it became my first challenge. One week without energy drinks or Diet Cokes. And to make matters worse, the only thing that worked for my headaches had just been recalled, and I couldn't find any anywhere.

"Remember the marathon?" I said quietly.

She nodded. Of course she remembered. She had been the one who'd helped me hobble around Disneyland the next day. "I tried to change then," I continued. "I thought running 26.2 miles would somehow fix everything. But it didn't. Because I didn't actually change anything. I just survived something hard and then went right back to the same life."

Andrea then asked, "So what's different this time?"

"This time, I'm not trying to prove something. I'm trying to become something. Someone different. Someone better."

She had already told me to try this for my headaches, but I acted as if I had come up with it on my own. "One week," I said. "No energy drinks. No Diet Coke. No Excedrin unless I absolutely can't function. Just . . . one week. And then we'll see."

"You know the headaches are going to get worse before they get better, right?" she said gently. "Caffeine withdrawal is real."

"I know."

"And you're going to be miserable for a few days."

"I know."

August 1, 2012. That's the date I drew my line in the sand.

No more Red Bull. No more Diet Coke. No more daily Excedrin. Cold turkey. The first three days were horrible. As Andrea had warned me, the headaches didn't just continue, they intensified. Withdrawal headaches stacked on top of my regular 3 p.m. headaches, creating a symphony of pain that made me question my sanity. But I didn't cave. Mainly because I couldn't get any Excedrin at the time.

Day four came, and the withdrawal fog started to lift. The headaches became less frequent. By day seven I woke up without a headache for the first time in months. Maybe years.

I walked into the kitchen, where Andrea was making breakfast for the boys, and I just stood there feeling . . . normal. Present. And awake.

"How do you feel?" she asked.

"It's crazy; I don't have a headache, and I actually feel pretty good."

She smiled and said, "I don't want to say I told you so, but I told you so."

The Transformation Begins

By week two, the headaches were completely gone. The afternoon crashes that used to send me reaching for another can of Red Bull had disappeared. I was more energetic than I had been in years, and it wasn't borrowed energy from energy drinks; it was real.

Andrea had been right, as usual. She had known for a long time what I finally had discovered: that the headaches weren't the problem. They were a symptom. The problem was a lifestyle that was broken.

One evening after the boys had gone to bed, Andrea and I were sitting on the couch. I was googling fitness challenges—old habits die hard; I had just replaced energy drinks with internet rabbit holes— and somehow I stumbled across something called an IRONMAN triathlon: swimming, biking, and running. The distances looked impossible, especially the swimming part, but there was something about it that wouldn't leave me alone. Maybe it was the challenge. Maybe it was how completely different it was from the sedentary life I had built. Or maybe it was that I needed something big enough to pull me away from who I had become.

I told Andrea about the idea of a triathlon.

She said, "Could you pick something that's not just about proving you can survive it? Something that makes you want to be healthy instead of just punishing yourself for not being healthy?" And she happily reminded me of the marathon catastrophe.

The marathon had turned out to be about punishment, about forcing my body to do something it wasn't prepared for. But what if this time could be different? What if it could be about building something instead of breaking something?

She then added, "Well, whatever you decide, maybe find someone who actually knows what they're doing. Someone who can teach you how to do it right."

That last part stuck with me. The marathon had failed partly because I had tried to do it alone, without guidance, without proper preparation. What if this time I found a mentor? What if I actually learned how to do something instead of just attempting it?

The Aquatic Center

A few days later, I was driving past the aquatic center, a building less than a mile from our house. I had passed the place hundreds of times without a second thought.

Swimming.

I swam as a kid. Backyard pools, beach vacations, a few lessons I barely remembered. How hard could it be to swim a few laps? I pulled into the parking lot and just sat there, staring at the glass entrance. This felt different than standing at the marathon starting line two years ago. That had felt like I was trying to prove something. This felt like I was trying to discover something.

What if I actually prepared this time? What if I found someone who knew what they were doing and learned from them? What if I treated this as a journey instead of an event?

The Beginning

Change often feels impossible. So many times, with good intentions, we make half-hearted attempts that last a few days or weeks, and then we slip back into old patterns. The journey of a thousand miles begins with a single step. But first, you have to be willing to admit you're not where you want to be.

That admission isn't failure; it's the first step toward becoming who you are meant to be. Your wake-up call might not come from a video screen. It might come from a conversation, a diagnosis, a mirror, or a quiet moment when you realize you've been living someone else's life. The question isn't whether that moment will come. It's what will you do when it does?

3

37 Yards and a Salad Bar

"You don't have to be great to start,
but you have to start to be great."
—ZIG ZIGLAR

N ow, standing in the parking lot in front of the aquatic center, gym bag in hand, I felt like I was about to cross into foreign territory.

It had been three weeks since my midnight wake-up call. Three weeks since I had quit the energy drinks and Diet Cokes. Three weeks since I'd decided that this time, unlike the marathon disaster, I would do this the right way.

When I walked through the glass doors, the smell hit me first, that sharp chlorine scent that takes you back to childhood pool parties and swimming lessons you barely remember. The sounds came next: the rhythmic splash of lap swimmers, the hum of pool filters, the echo of voices bouncing off high ceilings.

At the front desk, I signed up for a monthlong pass. The woman handed me a punch card and smiled. "First time?"

"Yes. Trying something new."

"Good for you. Pool's through those doors. Have fun."

Fun. Right.

I headed to the locker room feeling like an impostor. Around me, real swimmers moved with purpose, pulling on goggles, adjusting swim caps, stretching muscles that looked like they actually knew what they were doing. These people had equipment. Technique. Confidence.

I had board shorts and desperation.

I changed quickly, keeping my head down, and walked onto the pool deck. The facility was impressive: a 25-yard pool divided into eight lanes, with swimmers of all ages cutting through the water at various speeds. Some moved like dolphins. Others looked more like me, trying to survive.

I picked an empty lane, second from the end, figuring I would attract less attention there. For a moment, I stood at the edge, watching the swimmer in the next lane glide effortlessly back and forth. She made it look so easy; smooth strokes, controlled breathing, perfect rhythm. How hard could this be? I'd swum before. That had to count for something. Water was water, right?

I jumped in.

I pushed off from the wall with confidence, arms cutting through the water, breathing to my right like I had seen the other swimmers do. Twenty-five yards to the other end. I could definitely handle that.

Halfway across, my arms started burning. By the time I touched the far wall, I was gasping, sucking in air like I had sprinted a mile. But I made it. Twenty-five yards down, like everyone else in the pool.

I turned around and pushed off for the return trip.

That's when reality hit.

Five yards in, my arms felt like lead. Ten yards and I couldn't catch my breath. My stroke technique, if you could call it that, fell apart completely. No rhythm, no efficiency, just desperate thrashing as I tried to keep my head above water. I knew I was in trouble. At 37 yards, 13 yards short of completing one full lap, I stopped. Not at the wall. In the middle of the lane.

I treaded water for a few seconds, gasping, hoping no one was watching. My heart hammered against my chest like it was trying to escape. Every muscle in my arms and shoulders screamed in protest. I was basically drowning in a public pool with a lifeguard 10 feet away. I had to grab the lane rope and pull myself hand-over-hand to the edge of the pool. I'm not making this up. Thirty-seven yards. That's how far Jason Millsaps, future IRONMAN finisher, could swim on his first day back in the water.

I hauled myself out and sat on the edge for a moment, trying to look casual while my body recovered from what felt like a near-death experience. I grabbed my towel and dried off, very aware that the woman in the next lane was still swimming laps with perfect form while I was sitting there defeated.

Around me, swimmers half my age and twice my age continued their steady laps, making it look effortless. I changed back into my street clothes and walked to the front desk, where the same woman who had checked me in looked up with that smile.

"All done already?"

"Yeah," I said, trying to sound casual, like I had totally planned to be at the pool for only nine minutes. "But I'll be back. And next time I'll stay longer."

She nodded encouragingly. "That's the spirit. Everyone starts somewhere."

Walking to my car, I felt the familiar weight of defeat settling over me. The same feeling I'd had after the marathon. The same feeling as after every failed diet I had attempted, every failed New Year's resolution, every time I'd tried to change and hadn't been able to sustain it.

Thirty-seven yards.

In a full IRONMAN triathlon, I would need to swim 4,224 yards. I had just completed less than 1 percent of that distance, and I'd nearly drowned doing it. Sitting in my car in the aquatic center parking lot, I did the math. To swim an IRONMAN distance, I would need to do what I had just done 114 more times. Without stopping. In open water. Possibly with waves and currents. That sounds easy. What was I thinking? That I could just decide to become an athlete at 30-some years old? That watching a few YouTube videos would somehow make me capable of extraordinary things? I couldn't even swim two laps in a heated, calm, lifeguard-protected pool.

But as I sat there, something else came over me. Something I hadn't felt in a long time. The strange satisfaction of having tried something hard. I'd shown up. I had gotten in the water. I had pushed myself to the point of failure and lived to tell about it. Most people never even get wet. And 37 yards, as pathetic as it sounded, was 37 more yards than I had swum the day before.

That night at dinner, Andrea asked how the swimming had gone.

"Terrible," I admitted. "I made it 37 yards and had to stop."

"Thirty-seven?!" she blurted out, as the boys laughed. "Well, are you going back?" she asked.

"Yeah," I said. "Tomorrow." And I meant it.

Here's what I was already beginning to understand: Starting isn't about being good. It's about being willing to be bad at something long enough to get better. The pool didn't care about my excuses. It didn't care that I was out of shape or that I had never trained for anything athletic in my adult life. It was what it was, a challenge waiting for someone brave enough to jump in.

Thirty-seven yards wasn't a failure. It was a measurement. A starting point. The first data point in what could become a much longer story. The question wasn't whether I was qualified to be there. The question was whether I was willing to go back tomorrow and try for 38 yards.

The next day, I went back. This time, I made it 50 yards before having to stop. Progress, even if microscopic. The day after that, 75. Each session, I would get in the water, swim as far as I could, rest, and repeat. Sometimes I managed two laps. Sometimes only one. But I kept showing up. I made it to a full 100 yards without stopping. Four laps. It felt like summiting Everest.

The Meeting

As I was just starting my daily pool sessions, I was having lunch at work when one of our guest pastors stopped by our office. We got to talking, and somehow the conversation turned to fitness.

"I actually just did an IRONMAN race a few months ago," he mentioned casually, as if people did IRONMAN races all the time.

I nearly choked on my sandwich. "An IRONMAN race? Like the full thing? Swimming, biking, running?"

He laughed. "Yeah. It was my eighth one, actually."

Eight. This guy had done eight IRONMAN races.

"Scott Bennefield," he said, extending his hand. "I'm one of the pastors at a church here in town."

We talked for another 15 minutes about training, racing, and what it takes to complete 140.6 miles in one day. I tried to play it cool, as if I knew what I was talking about, but inside I was fascinated. Here was someone who had actually done the thing I was just googling about. This was a regular guy with a family and a job (like mine), and someone who had somehow completed eight IRONMAN races.

If he could do it . . .

I pushed the thought away. Let's not get ahead of ourselves. I was still celebrating swimming 100 yards without stopping. A full IRONMAN race was so far beyond my current abilities that thinking about it felt ridiculous. But the seed was planted.

After Scott left, I immediately looked him up online. There were photos of him crossing finish lines, articles about his races, and his church's website listing him as one of the pastors. I clicked on his email address listed and wrote a message:

Hey Scott, we just met when you were at my church. I saw where you also coached athletes. I'm new to swimming and triathlon, and I would love to meet for lunch sometime to hear about your journey and maybe get some advice. No pressure if you're too busy. Thanks for considering.

I hit send before I could overthink it.

He responded the next morning: *Jason, would love to meet. How about Sweet Tomatoes this Thursday at noon?*

Sweet Tomatoes. A salad bar. Of course a guy who'd done eight IRONMAN races would pick a salad bar.

The Salad Bar

Thursday arrived, and I was more nervous than I had been for any job interview or church presentation. I arrived early and sat in my car, watching for Scott. At exactly noon, a blue Mustang pulled into the parking lot. The bumper sticker: "8X IRONMAN Finisher."

Would I ever have a bumper sticker like that? Right now I would settle for "Successfully Completed a Quarter-Mile Swim Without Dying."

Scott got out of his car. He was fit but not intimidating, with the lean build of someone who spent serious time training but also the friendly demeanor of someone who genuinely wanted to help. We walked into the restaurant together, and I followed him through the salad bar line like a student shadowing a master. He loaded his plate with greens, vegetables, and a small amount of pasta. I copied his choices, pretending I ate like this all the time instead of living off whatever was quick and convenient.

We found a booth, and the conversation started casually. Families, ministry, life in Albuquerque. He was easy to talk to, which helped calm my nerves. Then we got to triathlon.

"So, what got you interested in this?" Scott asked.

I told him the abbreviated version: the wake-up call, giving up energy drinks, needing to change, stumbling across IRONMAN racing online. I confessed that I had just started swimming again and had barely been able to swim 37 yards the first time out, but was already up to a quarter mile.

"That's great progress," he said, and he meant it. No condescension, no judgment. Just genuine encouragement.

"My goal is to do a short triathlon," I said. "But eventually I think I want to do an IRONMAN 70.3 race. There's no way I could do a full-distance one."

Scott mentioned that there was a sprint triathlon coming up in late September in Santa Fe. "It's only a 200-yard swim, an 11-mile bike, and a 5K run."

That actually felt manageable.

Scott encouraged me, saying, "This would be a great first goal. Very realistic."

We talked through what training for a sprint tri would look like, balancing three sports, learning transitions, managing time with family and work responsibilities.

Then Scott said something that changed everything: "You know, after you do the sprint tri, if you want to keep going, I would be happy to coach you. I know you mentioned working toward an IRONMAN 70.3, but if you trained properly, you could do a full IRONMAN race."

I laughed. "I don't think so. I can barely swim half a mile, and I don't even own a bike."

"You could do it," he repeated. "Let me help you train, and we can both do IRONMAN Arizona next year."

I stared at him like he was crazy.

IRONMAN Arizona. That was 13 months away. Thirteen months to go from a guy who could barely swim a quarter mile to someone capable of 140.6 miles in one day? But something in his confidence, in his belief that I could do this, made me want to believe it too. The smart response would have been "Let me think about it." Or "Maybe I should do a few shorter races first." Or "That's too big a jump." Instead, I heard myself say, "Let's do this. We've got 13 months."

Where did that confidence come from? I have no idea. In that moment, sitting across from Scott at a salad bar in Albuquerque, something shifted. This wasn't about getting healthy anymore. This was about chasing something impossible and seeing if I could make it possible. That's when Scott became my coach, and someone who saw potential in me long before I could see it in myself.

As we finished lunch and walked back to our cars, Scott said, "Just keep showing up. That's the secret. Most people quit before they give themselves a chance to get good. But you're showing up every day. That's what matters."

Driving back to the office, I realized something had shifted. I wasn't just a guy flailing around in a pool anymore. I had a goal—a goal that was approaching really fast: the Santa Fe sprint triathlon in late September. And I had a coach who had actually done what I was dreaming about. For the first time since that midnight wake-up call, I felt like I was on a path instead of just wandering.

The next few weeks became a blur of training. Swimming at the aquatic center every morning. Riding the cheap aluminum bike I had just bought on Amazon. Running short distances, building up slowly, trying not to repeat the marathon disaster.

Andrea watched this new routine. "You're really doing this," she said one evening.

"Yes, I am. I'm not messing around."

"I'm proud of you," she said. "And a little worried you've lost your mind."

"Both can be true," I replied.

She laughed. "Just promise me you won't show up unprepared like you did for the marathon. Actually train this time. Listen to Scott. Do it right."

"Oh, I will."

Race Day Approaches

September arrived faster than expected. The Santa Fe sprint triathlon was two weeks away, and I was as ready as I was going to be. I could swim 200 yards easily now. I had ridden my bike on routes up to 20 miles. I could run a 5K without my legs falling apart. Individually, I could do all three disciplines. But could I do them back-to-back, in one race, without collapsing? There was only one way to find out.

Scott and I met the week before the race to go over final details— what race morning would look like, how to set up my transition area, how to pace myself.

"Remember," he said, "this is just your first one. The goal is to finish and learn. Don't worry about your time. Just execute what you've trained for and have fun."

Fun. There was that word again.

But this time, I thought maybe it actually could be fun. Because unlike the marathon, I had prepared for this. I had a plan. I had a coach. And I had done the work.

Race Day

Race morning arrived with my alarm going off at 3 a.m., a time I once believed existed only in theory. I ate my prerace meal (oatmeal with peanut butter and a banana), loaded my gear bags, and made the drive north to Santa Fe with a Clif Bar in one hand and too much nervous energy in my system.

The race site was chaotic in the best way possible. Athletes were everywhere, setting up transition areas, doing warm-up swims, nervously checking and rechecking their gear. I found my assigned spot in the transition area and carefully laid out everything exactly as I had practiced: bike shoes on the ground pointing toward the exit, helmet resting on handlebars already open and ready, sunglasses inside the helmet, race belt with my bib number already attached, running shoes and socks waiting nearby. I had practiced this setup a few times in my driveway. Muscle memory would handle the rest.

Body marking came next. A volunteer with a permanent marker wrote my race number on both arms and my age on my calf. I was official now.

The swim was serpentine style, down one lane, back the next, repeat. We lined up by placing ourselves in order of our projected swim times. I was optimistic in my estimate and somehow ended up as swimmer number nine out of 130 athletes. I started to quickly second-guess my projected time, or maybe I was the fastest triathlete at this race. Directly in front of me in line was a guy who'd qualified for the 2004 Olympic time trials. My fastest-triathlete theory immediately vanished. I knew I was in trouble the moment he dove in and glided through the water like he'd been born aquatic.

When my turn quickly came, I launched into the water with all the grace of someone who'd learned to swim a few weeks ago. The first lap went okay. The second lap, I started to panic, swallowing water, gasping for air, completely forgetting the technique I had practiced hundreds of times.

Swimmers behind me were passing on both sides. Some even went over me. I looked like someone who had never been in a pool before, much less trained for this moment.

But I kept going. Survival swimming, maybe, but still swimming.

When I finally climbed out of the pool, my lungs burned and my arms felt like overcooked pasta. But I was alive, and the hardest part was behind me.

I jogged into transition, found my gear, and pulled on socks with shaking hands. The bike mount line was crowded with athletes, some moving smoothly, others, like me, looking slightly disoriented. I mounted my bike and started pedaling.

The bike course wound through the high desert around Santa Fe, elevation 6,700 feet. The altitude made every breath feel insufficient, but the scenery was stunning, rolling hills backed by mountains, clear blue sky, and the kind of expansive landscape that makes you feel small in the best way. Eleven miles later, I rolled back into transition, dismounted, and racked my bike. My legs felt like foam noodles as I started the run, but gradually they remembered what to do.

The 5K felt longer than any training run had, probably because I swam and biked first. But I kept moving, walking the hills, running the flats, and somehow crossing the finish line in one piece. Official time: 1:16:14. I finished. My first triathlon was completed. First race combining all three disciplines. First proof that maybe Scott had been right; maybe I actually could do this.

The postrace awards ceremony brought an unexpected surprise. They called age-group winners to the podium, and I heard my name: "Second place, men's 30–35 age group: Jason Millsaps." Second place. In my first triathlon. I walked to the podium in disbelief and accepted a small medal that meant more than any participation trophy from childhood ever had. This wasn't given to me. This was earned.

That medal joined the others on my dresser mirror, but it held a different weight. This one represented not only finishing, but actually competing. Actually succeeding. I learned that transformation doesn't happen at finish lines. It happens in all the small moments between deciding to change and actually changing. It happens at 37 yards when you decide to come back for 38 yards. It happens when you find someone who believes in you before you believe in yourself. It happens when you stop treating challenges as punishments and start treating them as invitations. The finish line in Santa Fe wasn't the end of anything. It was just the beginning.

The Lesson

Starting is hard because it requires admitting you're not good at something yet. But "yet" is the most important word in that sentence. Every expert was once a beginner. Every champion was once a novice. Every finish line was once just a dream. The distance between who you are and who you could become isn't measured in talent or genetics. It's measured in the willingness to start, to practice, to fail, to improve, and to keep showing up.

Your first race, whatever that means for you, might not go perfectly. You might make mistakes, struggle, wonder if you belong there. But if you finish, you'll discover something valuable: You're capable of more than you thought. And that knowledge changes everything.

4

The 13-Month Journey

*"Success is the sum of small efforts
repeated day in and day out."*
—ROBERT COLLIER

In September 2012, I crossed my first triathlon finish line in Santa Fe, and something had shifted. I wasn't just a guy who had quit drinking energy drinks and Diet Cokes. I wasn't just someone trying to get healthy. I was a triathlete. And more than that, I had a coach who believed I could do something I still thought was impossible. Driving home from Santa Fe, I replayed the conversation with Scott at Sweet Tomatoes. He had said we could do IRONMAN Arizona together. Thirteen months away. November 2013.

I did the math in my head. That was:

- 2.4-mile swim (I had just done 200 yards.)
- 112-mile bike (I had just done 11 miles.)
- 26.2-mile marathon (I had barely survived one of these just two years earlier.)

The gap between where I was and where I needed to be felt astronomical. But Scott had done this eight times. He knew something I didn't. Maybe, just maybe, it was possible. When I got home, Andrea was putting the boys to bed. I waited until they were asleep, then joined her in the living room.

"So, how'd it go?" she asked, though my grin probably answered the question.

"I got second place in my age group."

"That's amazing! How many people were in your age group?"

I laughed. "Well . . . two. But still. Second place is second place."

She laughed. "I'm still proud of you. You actually did it. You trained, you finished, and you didn't destroy your body in the process."

"There's something else," I said. "Scott thinks I should do IRONMAN Arizona. Next November. Thirteen months from now."

Andrea pulled back and looked at me. "A full IRONMAN race? Like 140 miles?"

"Technically, it's 140.6."

"Jason . . ."

"I know it sounds crazy. But Scott's done eight of them. He will coach me. He believes I can do it."

She was quiet for a moment, and I could see her processing what this would mean. More training. Longer workouts. Early mornings and weekend rides that would take half the day.

"What do you think?" I asked.

"I think you're still crazy, but if this is what you want to do, then go do it!" she said.

"Scott will design me a training plan," I said. "A real one. Thirteen months of structured workouts. Building slowly. Doing it right. And I'll make sure it doesn't take over our lives. I've already decided that I will go to bed when you go to bed and train early in the morning before work. I won't miss important family stuff."

Andrea studied my face. "You really want this."

"I really do. But not if it means sacrificing our family. You and the boys come first. Always."

She took a deep breath. "Okay. But we're doing this together."

I looked at her, surprised. "You want to do an IRONMAN race too?!"

"Negative. I'll stay on the side and be the cheerleader!" she said.

"Deal. And I love you."

The Plan

The next day, I called Scott and told him I was in. He started loading my training plan that evening—a detailed, month-by-month schedule that would take me from sprint triathlete to IRONMAN finisher.

Looking at it spread across my computer screen, I felt both excited and terrified. This was real. This was happening. This was going to be the hardest thing I had ever attempted.

But this time, I wouldn't be doing it alone.

Scott's philosophy was simple: *We start where you are, and we finish together.*

My new weekly schedule looked like this:

- Monday: Strength training, Bike (60 minutes)
- Tuesday: Swim (45 minutes), Run (45 minutes)
- Wednesday: Bike (60 minutes)
- Thursday: Strength training, Run (45 minutes)
- Friday: Bike (60 minutes), Swim (45 minutes)
- Saturday: Run (45 minutes)
- Sunday: Rest and church

The alarm went off at 4:30 a.m. six days a week. I quietly got out of bed while Andrea and the boys slept, grabbed the workout clothes I had laid out the night before, and headed out into the dark Albuquerque morning.

Swimming remained my weakest discipline, but I was slowly improving. My stroke became smoother. My breathing became more efficient. The quarter mile that had once felt impossible now felt routine. I was working toward a full mile without stopping; still far from the 2.4 miles I would need for IRONMAN, but progress nonetheless.

Biking was where I found unexpected joy. There's something peaceful about long rides through the New Mexico desert. The rhythm of pedaling, the scenery, the simple pleasure of covering distance under your own power. Friday morning rides became my therapy, time to think, pray, process the week, and just be.

I mapped out several routes around Albuquerque, gradually extending the distance. Twenty miles became 30. Thirty became 40. My cheap Amazon bike wasn't fancy, but it worked. Other cyclists would pass me on carbon fiber road bikes that cost more than my car, but I didn't care. I was just grateful to be out there, moving forward.

Andrea had been right about the time commitment. A two- and then three-hour bike ride meant she was managing the boys alone for half the day. I tried to make up for it by taking over making dinner most nights to try to give her a little break, but let's be honest, moms don't ever really get a break! Sometimes I could see the strain. This was hard on her, but she never complained. I also tried to bring her flowers almost every week, which I still do to this day. However, I still owe her a lot more flowers after all these years!

The Move

Just as I was settling into a consistent training routine in Albuquerque, life threw us a curveball. A church in Athens, Georgia, had reached out asking me to consider coming to be their worship pastor. After several meetings, visits, and a lot of prayer and discussion, Andrea and I made the decision: We were moving to Athens, Georgia.

My new triathlon hobby was just that, a hobby. My real job was being a worship pastor. But the timing felt terrible. I was a couple of months into training for IRONMAN Arizona, finally had a rhythm with Scott's coaching, knew every running and bike route in Albuquerque. Starting over in a new city seemed like it could derail everything.

But Andrea saw it differently. "Maybe this is good timing," she said as we packed boxes. "New city, new start. You're not the same person who arrived in Albuquerque. You're bringing a new version of yourself to Athens."

She was right. The guy moving to Athens wasn't the Red Bull–addicted worship pastor who had failed at the marathon. He was someone who woke up at 4:30 a.m. without an alarm, who swam a mile before breakfast, who had quit chemicals cold turkey and never looked back.

Athens, Georgia

We loaded the moving truck in late 2012 and made the cross-country drive. Jonathan was seven now, Jaden almost four, old enough to understand we were starting fresh, young enough to be excited about the adventure.

The first week in Athens was unpacking boxes, starting a new job, getting Jonathan enrolled in school, meeting people, and learning our way around an unfamiliar city. But even in the chaos, I had to find places to train.

I joined a gym and a pool within two miles of our new house. It wasn't as nice as the aquatic center in Albuquerque, but it had lanes and water, and that's what mattered. The front-desk staff didn't know me yet, didn't know about my 37-yard beginning or my journey. I was just another guy buying a membership.

But within a few weeks, the staff at the new gym started recognizing me. "You're here almost every morning," one of them commented. "Training for something?"

"An IRONMAN race," I said, still getting used to saying it out loud.

"Wow. That's intense. Good luck."

Finding bike routes was pretty easy. There were many country roads around our house with rolling hills and winding, tree-lined streets. The terrain was very different from Albuquerque, with more elevation gains and more turns. My weekend rides became explorations, discovering routes through the Georgia countryside.

Scott was still coaching me remotely, uploading training plans via our training app and checking in weekly by phone. The distance didn't matter; he was committed to getting me to Arizona, no matter where I lived.

"How's the new city treating you?" he asked during one of our calls.

"We love it. Really green. Lots of hills, which is different from New Mexico."

"Hills are good training. They'll make you stronger for Arizona."

The Bike Shop

One Saturday morning, we were driving through downtown Athens when I passed a bike shop. Not a big-box sporting goods store, but a real cycling shop with high-end road bikes in the window and mechanics working in the back.

I had been riding my $200 Amazon bike for five months now. It worked, but barely. The gears slipped, the seat was uncomfortable on long rides, and I was constantly making adjustments. We pulled into the parking lot and walked inside.

The shop smelled like rubber and chain lubricant. Rows of sleek carbon fiber bikes lined the walls, with price tags that made me do a double take. A guy behind the counter looked up.

"Can I help you?"

"Hey, I'm training for an IRONMAN race," I said. "I need a real bike."

He smiled. "What are you riding now?"

"Um, I don't know the brand, but an aluminum bike I bought on Amazon for $200."

"And how's that working out?"

"It gets me from point A to point B. Barely."

He laughed. "Let's get you set up properly."

For the next hour, he walked me through options. We talked about bike geometry, frame materials, and aerodynamics. He then scheduled me to come in the next week for a custom bike fit.

I went back the next week, and he had several options for a midrange triathlon bike. He rolled out a black and red Specialized bike. "Here's what I would recommend for someone doing their first IRONMAN race," he said. "It's not the cheapest option, but it's reliable and comfortable, and it will last you through many races." I looked at the price tag. It was more than I had ever spent on anything that wasn't a car or furniture. But this was an investment in the goal. This was fully committing.

"I'll take it," I said.

Andrea's face when I brought it home was a mix of shock and resignation. "That's a really nice bike."

"It's sweet!" I had already called her before we purchased it to tell her the price. I said, "It's a lot of money—"

"It's fine," she said. "You're doing this. You might as well do it right."

The First Ride

Before taking my bike outside for my first ride, I practiced clipping in and out of the pedals. I leaned up against the garage door and clipped in and out over and over. It was a weird feeling at first, being locked to your pedals. I finally left the driveway and took it out on the road. The first ride on my new bike was transformative. The gears shifted smoothly. The geometry fit my body perfectly. The weight was significantly lighter than that of my Amazon special. I felt fast, even though I probably wasn't actually much faster.

Now, riding through Athens on a proper triathlon bike, custom fitted to my body, I felt different. I felt like someone who belonged. Like maybe I actually was an athlete, not just someone pretending to be one.

That evening, Andrea found me in the garage, cleaning my new bike.

"You really love this, don't you?" she said.

"I do. Is that weird?"

"No. It's actually really great. I was worried when we moved that you would lose your momentum. But you're more committed than ever."

"You know if I put my mind to something, I will finish it," I said.

"Oh yes, I know. I'm so proud of you."

The Next Step

With the move to Athens behind us and my training back on track, I registered for IRONMAN 70.3 Florida in Haines City, May 26, 2013. That gave me seven weeks to prepare for 1.2 miles of swimming, 56 miles of biking, and a 13.1-mile half-marathon. Scott's plan ramped up significantly. Four-hour weekend rides. Mile-and-a-half swims. Long runs that left my legs useless for the rest of the day.

The final week before Florida, I started looking over every detail. What should I pack? How early should we leave for Florida? What if I forget something critical?

I made lists. Checked them twice. Made new lists. Laid out all my gear in the living room and took photos to reference later.

Jonathan walked by and looked at the gear spread across the floor. "Dad, that's a lot of stuff for one race."

"I know, buddy. But I need all of it."

"Why do you do this?" he asked. "It seems really hard."

I thought about his question. Why was I doing this? What was the point of all this suffering, all this sacrifice?

"Because I want to show you something," I said. "I want you to see that anyone, people like your dad, can do really hard things if they don't give up. And that you should finish what you start."

He nodded, processing. "Are you going to finish?"

"I'm going to try really hard."

"Good," he said, then went back to playing.

The Journey

The next morning, we loaded into the car for the drive to Haines City. Athens to Florida. A family trip built around a race that still seemed impossible. I was someone who showed up. Someone who kept promises to himself. Someone who didn't quit when things got hard. The race would be the test. But the transformation had already happened.

5

Cold-Water Awakening

"Only those who will risk going too far can possibly find out how far one can go."
—T. S. ELIOT

The sprint triathlon in Santa Fe had given me false confidence. Swimming in a heated, chlorinated pool with clear lane lines and a wall to push off from every 25 yards? That was manageable. Even easy, after months of practice. But open-water swimming, the kind I would face in a real triathlon, was something else entirely. And I was about to learn that lesson the hard way.

We had moved from Albuquerque to Athens, Georgia. New city, new house, new routines. But one thing remained constant: I was still training. Still chasing the dream of completing a full IRONMAN. Scott was still coaching me remotely, and I had found new places to swim, bike, and run.

With IRONMAN Arizona now less than seven months away, Scott's training plan had ramped up significantly. The workouts were longer, harder, more specific. And looming on the calendar was something I had been both anticipating and dreading: my first open-water swim race.

Race Registration

I registered for the John Tanner Sprint Triathlon in Carrollton, Georgia, about two hours west of our new home in Athens. The race would be held at a state park with a lake swim, which meant I would finally face the challenge every IRONMAN athlete must overcome: swimming in murky water with no walls, no lane lines, and no lifeguards standing poolside.

The night before the race, I laid out all my gear with precision. Tri suit, check. Goggles, check. Race belt, check. Bike shoes, socks, running shoes, gels, water bottles, sunscreen, towel, sandals—everything had its place.

I took the obligatory photo of my gear spread and posted it to social media with some motivational caption about being ready. But the truth was, I felt uneasy in ways I hadn't before Santa Fe. Something about open-water swimming scared me in a way pool swimming never had.

Race Morning

Race morning arrived at 3 a.m., as race mornings always do. I ate my standard prerace breakfast—oatmeal with peanut butter and a banana—and loaded the car while trying not to wake Andrea and the boys. The drive to Carrollton took over two hours, and I arrived at the park right as the sun was beginning to paint the sky with streaks of pink and orange.

I checked in, got my body marked with my race number and age group, and made the mandatory six trips to the porta-potty that every nervous athlete makes before a race. Then I walked down to the lake to see what I was getting into.

The first thing I noticed was the temperature. The volunteer at the check-in table had cheerfully announced, "Water temp is 67.8 degrees Fahrenheit this morning! Wetsuit legal!" The second thing was that everyone, and I mean everyone, was wearing a wetsuit.

Everyone except me.

I stood on the shoreline in my basic tri suit, watching hundreds of athletes zip themselves into thick neoprene armor. They were applying Body Glide and anti-chafing products, helping each other with zippers, moving with the practiced efficiency of people who knew exactly what they were doing.

I had never even worn a wetsuit. I didn't even own one. In all my research and preparation, somehow I had missed this crucial detail: When water temperatures drop below 76.1 degrees, wetsuits aren't just allowed, they're practically mandatory. They provide buoyancy, reduce drag, and most importantly, keep you from freezing.

I tried to play it cool, standing there like I had intentionally chosen to go without. Like I was some hardcore Northerner used to swimming in ice-cold waters. In reality, I was the idiot who didn't know better.

Sometimes you're underprepared. Sometimes you don't have the right gear. But showing up anyway is how growth begins, even if growth comes with mild hypothermia.

The swim start was organized by wave, with age groups entering the water at five-minute intervals. I lined up with the other men in my age group, watching the earlier waves charge into the lake with varying degrees of grace and panic.

The starting horn sounded for my wave, and suddenly 200 people were running into the water like we were storming a beach. I hit the water and immediately understood why everyone was wearing wetsuits. The cold shocked my system like I had been electrified. My lungs seized. My chest tightened. I couldn't catch my breath. The frigid water stole the air from my body, and for a terrifying moment, I thought I might not be able to swim at all.

I pushed forward anyway, with my head now above water, trying to find my stroke, but the chaos around me made it impossible. Arms and legs thrashed everywhere. Someone kicked my back. Another swimmer slapped my goggles sideways. I got dunked underwater by someone swimming over me. This wasn't a race, it was a survival scenario.

I stopped swimming and began treading water, letting the pack surge ahead while I tried to calm my breathing and adjust to the temperature. My heart was hammering at what felt like 300 beats per minute. My body was in full panic mode.

That's when I remembered something from my music background. When I'm anxious or stressed, humming helps regulate my breathing and calm my nervous system. It sounds ridiculous, but in that moment of near panic, it was the only tool I had. I put my face in the water and started humming underwater. I don't even remember what tune; it didn't matter. The rhythm of it, the vibration in my chest, the familiar sensation reminded me I was still in control, still capable of moving forward. Slowly, my heart rate dropped. My breathing steadied. I found my stroke again and started making progress through the dark, murky water.

Six hundred yards of open-water swimming is only about 12 laps in a pool. But in a cold lake with limited visibility, no walls to rest on, and the constant battle against my own panic, it felt like miles.

Twenty-eight minutes later, I stumbled out of that lake like a newborn calf learning to walk. My legs were shaking from the cold and adrenaline. My arms felt like rubber. But I was alive, and more importantly, I had survived my first open-water swim.

I ran to the transition area and found my bike on the rack, which was easy since almost everyone was on their bike by this time. My hands were shaking so badly I could barely get my socks on. I fumbled with my bike shoes, nearly dropped my helmet, and wondered if I would ever feel warm again. But once I was on the bike, everything changed.

The movement generated warmth. The morning sun began to burn through the clouds. My legs remembered what to do, and the 12-mile course gave me enough time to recover from the swim trauma before starting the run.

The run felt surprisingly strong. My body was cooperating, my pace was steady, and I actually enjoyed running the 5K. When I crossed the finish line, I checked my watch: 1:16:14.

I hadn't had any time expectations or goals, I just wanted to finish, but given the cold-water disaster, I was happy with my time.

The Debrief

Driving home that afternoon, still wrapped in a jacket despite the Georgia heat, I reflected on what I had learned. The obvious lesson was: Buy a wetsuit before the next race. But the deeper lesson was about adaptability.

I had gone into that race underprepared. I had faced a challenge I wasn't equipped for. And instead of quitting or making excuses, I had found a way to adapt. The humming technique that had calmed my panic wasn't in any training manual; it was something I'd improvised in the moment because I refused to give up.

Leadership, whether in athletics, business, or life in general, often requires improvisation. You can't always be perfectly prepared. Sometimes you show up with the wrong gear, facing conditions you didn't expect, and you have to figure it out in real time.

The question isn't whether you'll face unexpected challenges. The question is: Will you adapt and keep moving forward, or will you let the cold water stop you before you've even started?

That evening, I called Scott to debrief.

"How'd it go?" he asked.

"The swim was a disaster. Twenty-eight minutes for 600 yards. I almost panicked. Everyone had wetsuits except me. The water was freezing."

"But you finished."

"Yeah."

"That's what matters. Now you know what open water feels like. You know you need a wetsuit. You know the panic is manageable. All of that is valuable information for Florida."

"I guess so."

"Jason, every race is a lesson. Some races teach you what to do. Some teach you what not to do. Sounds like this one taught you both."

That night, I ordered a wetsuit online. It arrived three days later, and I immediately drove to the pool to practice swimming in it. The difference was remarkable: instant buoyancy, warmth, and a feeling of actually being equipped for what I was trying to do.

But I never forgot that cold morning in Carrollton. The fear, the panic, the moment I had to choose between quitting and finding a way forward. Seven months later, when I stood on the shore of Tempe Town Lake in Arizona, preparing for my first full IRONMAN, I would need to remember that lesson: You don't have to be perfectly prepared. You have to be willing to adapt and keep swimming.

Even when the water is cold. Even when you're scared. Even when everyone else seems better equipped than you. Just keep swimming.

The Lesson

A few weeks later, standing on the beach in Haines City, Florida, about to start my first IRONMAN 70.3, I would remember that cold morning in Carrollton. The panic, the fear, the moment I had to choose between quitting and finding a way forward.

The lesson John Tanner taught me wasn't just about wetsuits or open-water technique. It was about the difference between being perfectly prepared and being willing to adapt. You will never be perfectly ready for every challenge. But if you're willing to improvise, to problem-solve in real time, to keep moving forward even when conditions aren't ideal, that's when growth happens.

I learned that morning that courage isn't the absence of fear. It's swimming through the fear toward the shore you can barely see. And six weeks later, I would need that lesson again, standing on another beach, preparing to swim 1.2 miles with hundreds of other athletes, all of us chasing something that once seemed out of reach.

The Questions

How do you respond when you realize you're underprepared for the challenge in front of you?

Do you retreat and wait for perfect conditions, or do you adapt and move forward with what you have?

The gap between those who accomplish extraordinary things and those who don't isn't always preparation; sometimes it's the willingness to improvise when preparation falls short.

What challenge are you facing right now for which you feel under-prepared or under-equipped?

Maybe the question isn't whether you're ready. Maybe the question is whether you're willing to jump in anyway and figure it out as you go.

Half the Distance,
Double the Fear

"It always seems impossible until it's done."
—NELSON MANDELA

The alarm went off at 3:30 a.m., pulling me from restless sleep into the darkness of our hotel room in Haines City, Florida. This was it. My first IRONMAN 70.3: 1.2 miles of swimming, 56 miles of biking, and a 13.1-mile run. All in one day. All without stopping.

When I started this journey, an IRONMAN 70.3 was the ultimate goal. The pinnacle. The thing I told Scott I wanted to accomplish "someday, maybe, possibly." A full IRONMAN? That was for other people—superhumans or crazy people.

But here I was, six months into training, about to attempt something that had once seemed as impossible as flying to the moon. And in a few months, I would be standing at the starting line of IRONMAN Arizona, attempting twice this distance. Somehow, what used to be my ceiling had become my foundation.

I rolled out of bed and went through my prerace routine with mechanical precision. Breakfast: granola with almond milk, yogurt, whole-grain waffles, and some kind of green juice that tasted like lawn clippings but supposedly provided nutrients. I had learned from Scott that race-day nutrition started in training and way before race day. Your body needed fuel for what was coming.

Andrea was already up, getting ready to spend the entire day tracking me and cheering at various points along the course. The boys were still asleep. We had made this a family trip, turning my race into a mini-vacation. After I finished (if I finished), we would spend a few days at the beach.

"How are you feeling?" Andrea asked, watching me methodically pack my transition bags.

"Scared half to death," I admitted.

She smiled. "You've got this."

I wished I shared her confidence.

We arrived at the race venue around 4:40 a.m. The park was already buzzing with nervous energy, hundreds of athletes moving through the darkness with headlamps, setting up transition areas, and doing last-minute bike checks.

I found my assigned spot in the transition area and dropped off my gear bags with one of the volunteers, who placed my bag in order by athlete number. Bike shoes positioned just right, helmet open and ready, nutrition bottles secured to my bike frame, running shoes and socks waiting for the second transition—T2. Every detail mattered. Every second counted.

After confirming that my bike was set and gear bags were dropped off, I walked toward the lake to see what I would be swimming in. That's when I saw them.

Signs. Everywhere.

"DO NOT SWIM—BEWARE OF ALLIGATORS"

I stopped and stared. We were about to jump into a lake with warning signs explicitly telling us not to do the very thing we had paid hundreds of dollars to do. The irony wasn't lost on me, but the fear was real.

I walked closer to the water's edge, where the sandy beach met the lake. The grass along the shore was tall, waist high in places, and thick. My mind immediately conjured images from every nature documentary I had ever watched.

The alligator slithers silently through the reeds, its eyes locked on unsuspecting prey entering the water . . .

And I was the prey. Wearing a hot pink swim cap (not my choice—they assigned colors by age group) and about to voluntarily enter gator territory.

Athletes began gathering on the beach. A young woman sang the national anthem, her voice carrying across the water as the sun began to rise. Race officials gave last-minute instructions about the course, cutoff times, and what to do in case of emergency.

Then came the final countdown.

Ten seconds.

My heart hammered against my chest. This was so much bigger than the sprint triathlon in Santa Fe or the cold-water disaster in Georgia. This was 70.3 miles. This was the distance that separated casual athletes from endurance athletes.

Five seconds.

I adjusted my goggles one last time.

The cannon fired.

It was a rolling start, four athletes entering the water every five seconds. The line moved quickly, and soon I was stepping onto the ramp that led into the lake. The tall grass brushed against my legs as I walked down, and all I could think about was alligators.

I positioned myself toward the back of my age group, having learned from previous races that starting too aggressively only led to chaos and exhaustion. Better to find my rhythm early and build from there.

The water wasn't too cold, almost lukewarm. At 78 degrees, it was non–wetsuit legal, which meant I was swimming in only my tri suit. The temperature was perfect, but the visibility was terrible. Dark, murky water where you couldn't see more than a foot below the surface.

The swim course had multiple turns that would require constant sighting to stay on course. I settled into my stroke, focusing on long, smooth pulls and steady breathing. Every few strokes, I would lift my head to sight the next buoy.

Around me, other swimmers found their paces. Some pulled ahead quickly. Others fell behind. I tried to stay focused on my own race, my own rhythm, trusting the training that had brought me here.

The course took us out into the lake, around several buoys, and back toward shore. At one point, I veered off course, an easy mistake when you can't see the bottom and the buoys are small dots in the distance. I corrected, adjusted, and kept swimming.

Forty-eight minutes after entering the water, I emerged onto the beach, grateful to be alive and uneaten by prehistoric reptiles.

Transition 1 was chaos in the best way. Volunteers called out numbers, helping athletes find their gear bags. I grabbed mine, jogged into the changing tent, and quickly transformed from swimmer to cyclist.

Socks on. Bike shoes laced. Helmet secured. Sunglasses in place. Energy gels taped to my bike frame in perfect formation for easy access. One bottle with sports drink, another with electrolyte tablets dissolved in water.

I had practiced this transition dozens of times, and muscle memory took over.

I grabbed my bike, jogged to the mount line, and swung my leg over. Fifty-six miles to go.

The bike course was mostly flat, which should have been a blessing. But Florida has a way of making "flat" deceptive with its constant wind and unrelenting sun. The heat built quickly, and by mile 20, I was already downing fluids and consuming gels on schedule.

Every 15 minutes, I drank. Every hour, I ate. The nutrition plan Scott had drilled into me was now automatic: sports drink, electrolyte tablets, and some energy gels. Three hours and 17 minutes after starting the bike, I rolled back into transition.

Transition 2 brought its own challenges. I dismounted, handed my bike to a volunteer, and grabbed my run gear bag. Inside the changing tent, I laced up my running shoes, grabbed my hat and race belt, and stumbled out into the sunlight.

My legs felt like they belonged to someone else. Heavy, uncoordinated, refusing to move the way they should. This was the brick effect times 10. I had done bike-to-run workouts in training, but nothing fully prepares you for starting a half-marathon after swimming and biking for over four hours.

I started running, or what passed for running. More of a shuffle, really. But I was moving forward, and that's what mattered.

The run course began with a steep hill. Everyone around me immediately walked it, so I joined them. No shame in walking when your legs feel like concrete and the sun is trying to melt you into the pavement.

I settled into a run-walk strategy: run the flats and downhills, walk the uphills and through aid stations. At every aid station, I grabbed ice to stuff down my tri suit, cold sponges to drape over my neck, and whatever fluids looked appealing.

The course wound through residential neighborhoods in Haines City, where locals stood at the ends of their driveways with garden hoses, offering to spray down overheated athletes. I accepted every single one.

Around mile 10, I heard the announcer's voice in the distance, calling out finishers. The sound gave me a surge of energy I didn't know I still had. I picked up my pace, pushing through the fatigue and pain.

Then I saw them, Andrea and the boys standing near the finish line, cowbells ringing, cheering like I was winning the whole race instead of just trying to finish.

I was going to finish. My first IRONMAN 70.3. The goal I had set six months ago when I could barely swim 37 yards.

I crossed the finish line with my hands raised. Official time: 6:52:17.

A volunteer draped a medal around my neck and handed me a bottle of cold water. I chugged it immediately, then grabbed another. My body was screaming for hydration.

I found Andrea and the boys in the crowd. They were beaming, proud, excited. I was exhausted, dehydrated, and already thinking about how much harder IRONMAN Arizona would be, twice this distance, in just seven months.

"You did it!" Andrea said, hugging me carefully, either because I looked like I might break or because I was covered in gallons of sweat and whatever mysterious substances live in that lake.

"I did," I said, still processing what I had just accomplished.

The Reflection

That night, I reflected on the journey, giving my family a play-by-play of the race. The distance that was my Everest six months ago was now a stepping stone to something even bigger.

Training for an IRONMAN 70.3 had transformed me. I had lost 40 pounds, built discipline I didn't know I had, and proven to myself that *impossible* was a word people use before they try.

But more than the physical changes, something deeper had shifted. I was beginning to understand that progress rarely comes suddenly. It comes from showing up daily, trusting the process, refusing to quit when it gets hard.

What had once seemed impossible had become possible.

And if this was possible, what else might be?

Seven months from now, I would find out.

The Questions

What was once your ceiling but has now become your foundation?

Sometimes the greatest gift of achieving a goal isn't the achievement itself; it's discovering you're capable of more than you thought.

Your IRONMAN 70.3 moment might not involve swimming with alligators or biking through Florida heat. It might be rebuilding after a divorce, starting over in a new career, finishing a degree while working full-time, or simply showing up for your life when everything in you wants to quit.

The distance doesn't matter. What matters is that you keep moving toward your finish line, even when the path is longer and harder than you imagined.

7

140.6 Miles of Faith

"It is hard to fail, but it is worse never to have tried to succeed."
—THEODORE ROOSEVELT

By November 2013, I had reached the moment Scott and I had been training for over the past 13 months. Thirteen months of waking up at 4 a.m. Thirteen months of swimming, biking, and running six days a week. Thirteen months of choosing discipline over comfort, training over sleep, preparation over convenience. And I had now lost 50 pounds!

The numbers were staggering when I looked back at my training log: more than 3,200 miles by bike, 660 miles on foot, and 211,000 yards in the pool. I had essentially biked from Athens, Georgia, to San Francisco, then another 700 miles up the coast toward Seattle, all on local roads and a stationary trainer.

But those numbers didn't capture the real preparation. They didn't show the mornings when my alarm went off and every fiber of my being wanted to stay in bed. They didn't measure the times Andrea managed the household alone while I was on a four-hour bike ride. They didn't account for the doubt that crept in during long runs, the voice that whispered I couldn't do this, wasn't built for this, should quit while I was ahead.

Thirteen months to prepare for one day.

One day that would either validate everything or expose me as someone who had aimed too high.

Andrea and I flew into Phoenix on Wednesday, three days before the race. As the plane descended, I gazed out the window, staring at Tempe Town Lake, where I would be swimming on Sunday. The reservoir looked impossibly small from this altitude, but I knew from studying the course map that it would feel plenty large when I was actually swimming in it.

We checked into our hotel and immediately fell into the prerace routine I had practiced for smaller races. Unpack. Organize gear. Check the bike, again. Review nutrition plan, again. Make lists. Check the lists.

The stakes felt higher. This wasn't just a race; this was the culmination of everything I had worked toward since that salad bar meeting with Scott.

"You're going to be fine," Andrea said, watching me lay out nutrition products for the third time.

"What if I'm not? What if I can't finish?"

"You will finish. You are too stubborn not to."

And I took that as a compliment.

Thursday brought athlete check-in at the expo. The athlete area was massive, vendors everywhere, athletes from around the world picking up race packets, the buzz of thousands of people about to attempt something most humans would never even consider.

I showed my ID, received my race packet with bib number and timing chip, and felt the weight of reality settling in. In three days, I would be racing 140.6 miles.

Scott met us at the expo. Seeing him brought immediate calm. He had done this before, multiple times. He knew what to expect, knew I was ready, knew that the panic I was feeling was normal.

"How are you feeling?" he asked.

"Terrified."

"Good. Everyone's terrified. That means you care."

Having a guide made everything feel more manageable.

That afternoon, we drove to Tempe Beach Park for the practice swim. Standing at the edge of Tempe Town Lake, looking at the clear water reflecting Arizona's blue sky, I felt the magnitude of what was coming.

I waded in with hundreds of other athletes, all of us testing the water temperature (62 degrees—wetsuit legal), getting comfortable with the swim course, trying to quiet our nerves. I swam a few hundred yards, enough to confirm I could handle it. The water felt good. My wetsuit worked perfectly. Everything seemed manageable.

But I knew race day would be different. Two thousand people churning the water, everyone fighting for position, the chaos of a mass start I hadn't yet experienced. I had only done wave starts, and those were chaotic enough.

Friday and Saturday blurred together in a haze of preparation. We drove the bike course so I could see every climb, every turn, every aid station. The course was three loops, which meant I would pass the same landmarks multiple times. That felt both comforting (familiar) and daunting (I have to do this *three* times?).

I racked my bike Saturday afternoon, going through the ritual of checking tire pressure, loading nutrition bottles, taping energy gels to my top tube in perfect formation. Everything had its place. Everything had been practiced.

Saturday night, I tried to sleep but mostly stared at the ceiling, running through the race in my mind. The swim start. The bike transition. The long miles on the bike. The marathon that would come when I was already exhausted.

At some point, I must have slept, because suddenly my alarm went off at 4:30 a.m.

Race day had arrived.

Race Day

I forced down breakfast—two packets of oatmeal, a banana, a bottle of sports drink—then gathered my gear and made my way to transition in the predawn darkness.

The energy was electric. Thousands of athletes moving through final preparations, volunteers shouting directions, the hum of organized chaos that precedes something significant.

I checked my bike one final time, loaded my special-needs bags onto the transport truck, and walked toward the swim start.

Andrea found me in the crowd. I gave her a kiss. This was it. Everything I had worked for was about to happen.

"I love you," she said.

"Love you too."

"You've got this."

I hoped she was right.

The pros started at 7 a.m., and I watched them explode into the water with efficiency I could only dream about. Then age groupers all entered the water.

I was standing with Scott, and we walked to the water's edge together, said a quick prayer—*Lord, give us strength. Keep us safe. Let us honor you in this race*—and waded into Tempe Town Lake.

The cannon fired, and suddenly I was swimming.

The swim was chaos, but controlled chaos. Two thousand arms and legs thrashing, everyone fighting for position, goggles getting kicked, bodies colliding. But I had expected this. I settled into a rhythm, focusing on long strokes and steady breathing.

I got elbowed. Someone kicked my goggles. Another swimmer climbed over my back. But I kept swimming, kept sighting the buoys, kept moving forward.

The course was down and back. I made the first turn, then second, and headed back to where we started. One hour and 25 minutes after entering the water, I exited the water.

T1 was organized chaos. I grabbed my bike gear bag, found a spot in the packed changing tent, and changed into my bike gear. Wetsuit off. Dry off. Bike shoes on. Helmet secured. Sunglasses. Race belt. Everything felt good.

I jogged out to grab my bike, and the volunteer at the sunscreen station stopped me. "Hold still," she said, smearing white sunscreen all over my exposed skin. I looked ridiculous but would thank her later when the Arizona sun was blazing. I grabbed my bike, jogged to the mount line, and swung my leg over. Thousands of spectators cheered like we were starting the Tour de France. I clipped in and started the 112-mile journey.

My nutrition plan was precise, taped to my bike stem for reference:

- Hour 1: Half bottle sports drink, half bottle electrolyte water
- Hour 2: PB&J sandwich, continue fluids
- Hour 3: Energy gel, fluids
- Hour 4: Pick up special-needs bag, refuel

I had practiced this plan dozens of times. Every 15 minutes, I sipped. Every hour, I ate. The plan was automatic now, ingrained through months of training.

The first loop felt strong. The Arizona morning was cool, the roads were smooth, and my legs felt fresh. I passed some cyclists, got passed by others. This was my race, my pace. Loop two brought fatigue but nothing unmanageable. I stayed disciplined with nutrition, kept hydrating, and kept moving forward. Then, on the third loop, around mile 95, I felt something wrong with my rear tire.

It was going flat.

I pulled over, trying not to panic. A volunteer appeared within seconds, one of the bike mechanics stationed along the course for exactly this situation. He helped me change the tube, and within five minutes I was back on the bike. Crisis averted. But 8 miles later, mile 103, the tire went flat again. This time, I had used my only spare tube. I had no backup plan. I had trained for mechanical issues, carried tools and a spare, but hadn't prepared for two flats in one race.

I got off my bike and started walking, calculating whether I could walk 9 miles and still make the bike cutoff time. Then, like an answer to prayer, a SAG (support and gear) vehicle appeared. The mechanic fixed my tire with their supplies, and I was back on the bike. But the damage was done. The two flats had cost me time and mental energy. My carefully constructed race plan felt like it was unraveling. I pushed through the final miles and crossed the timing mat at T2, relieved that it was now all behind me.

The bike-to-run transition was a blur. I grabbed my run gear bag, changed shoes on legs that barely functioned, and stumbled out onto the marathon course. The first few steps were terrible, the infamous brick effect of trying to run after 112 miles on a bike. My legs felt like they belonged to someone else, heavy and uncooperative. But I had trained for this. I knew the feeling would pass. I had to keep moving.

I settled into a run-walk pattern: run to the next aid station, walk through while consuming fluids and food, run to the next one. This wasn't about speed anymore. It was about forward progress.

The Arizona sun climbed higher, and the temperature rose. At every aid station, I grabbed ice to stuff down my shirt and cold sponges to drape over my neck, and took in more fluids.

Around mile 14, an aid station volunteer handed me a cup of warm chicken broth. It sounded disgusting. It tasted amazing. That sodium gave me strength I didn't know I needed.

By mile 20, I was hurting. But I kept moving. One foot in front of the other.

Then, around mile 23, I looked at my watch and realized that if I pushed through this pain, I could finish in under 14 hours.

That thought ignited something inside me. I picked up my pace, running more than I had in miles, pushing through exhaustion and pain.

Mile 24. Mile 25. Mile 26.

And then I saw it: the finish line.

The lights, the crowd. The announcer, Mike Reilly, a.k.a. "the Voice of IRONMAN," was calling names as finishers crossed. I could hear individual names now, getting closer with each step.

I turned onto the red carpet of the finish chute. And then I heard it, the words I had been waiting 13 months to hear:

"Jason Millsaps, from Athens, Georgia . . . YOU ARE AN IRONMAN!"

I crossed the finish line with both arms raised.

Official time: 13:54:15.

A volunteer caught me, asked if I was okay, draped a medal around my neck, and wrapped me in a space blanket.

The Realization

I did it. After 13 months of training. After giving up energy drinks and transforming my life. After swimming 37 yards and nearly quitting. After that salad bar meeting with Scott.

I was an IRONMAN finisher.

I found Andrea in the finisher area, and we hugged. She'd had a front-row seat, watching me train for over a year. She had believed in me when I didn't believe in myself.

"You did it," she said.

"We did it," I corrected. Because this medal belonged to both of us.

Thirteen months of sacrifice had led to this one day. But more than the medal, more than the finish time, I had proven to myself: When you commit fully to something, when you show up even when it's hard, when you refuse to quit despite obstacles and doubts, the unthinkable becomes achievable.

I'm not claiming the race itself is a spiritual act or that God cares about my finish time, but I keep learning and experiencing that faith sustains us beyond our capabilities; that discipline prepares you for the finish line, but faith carries you when strength runs out. Every flat tire, every moment of doubt, every painful step—none of it was wasted. It all prepared me for the moment when I needed to dig deeper than training could take me. That's when faith takes over. And faith carried me 140.6 miles.

The Questions

What "IRONMAN race" are you training for in your own life?

What impossible thing is calling you to prepare, to show up, to refuse to quit?

The distance doesn't matter. What matters is the daily discipline, the commitment to keep going when everything says stop, and the faith that carries you when your strength runs out.

Your finish line is waiting. The only question is: Will you show up for the training required to reach it?

PART II

THE
MIDDLE
MILES

8

When Races Break You

"Sometimes you win, sometimes you learn."
—JOHN C. MAXWELL

Not every race goes according to plan. In fact, most don't. Between my first IRONMAN in Arizona (2013) and my eventual journey to Kona (2024), I learned that the races that break you often teach you more than the races that go well. Two races in particular, IRONMAN Louisville in August 2014 and IRONMAN Texas in May 2015, taught me what happens when conditions, preparation, and reality collide in ways you can't control.

IRONMAN Louisville was nothing more than a heat demon. Andrea and I drove from Athens to Louisville on Thursday, giving ourselves two full days before the race to settle in, scout the course, and adjust. Louisville in late August is beautiful. The Ohio River cuts through the city of historic neighborhoods, baseball history, and horses. We checked in to our hotel and headed straight to the expo for athlete check-in.

Friday morning, we went to the Ohio River for the mandatory practice swim. The water was brown and murky, and smelled like a river that runs through industrial cities. The volunteer cheerfully announced: "Water temperature this morning is 88 degrees!"

Eighty-eight degrees. Too warm for wetsuits, which meant we would be swimming in only our tri suits.

That evening, Andrea and I drove the entire 112-mile bike course. The route went through the rolling hills of Kentucky countryside.

Race Day

Race morning arrived with thick humidity. The weather for the day was predicted to be in the mid- to upper 90s with humidity near 100 percent. Heat index well over 100 degrees. This was going to be brutal.

The swim was rough but doable. Out of the water in a respectable time, feeling good, ready to tackle the bike. T1 went smoothly. I changed quickly, grabbed my bike, and rolled out onto the streets of Louisville welcomed by cheers from spectators lining the road.

The first hour felt great. My legs were fresh, my nutrition was on schedule, and the morning air was still relatively cool. I settled into a comfortable pace, enjoying the scenery of Kentucky horse country. Then the sun came out.

By mile 30, the temperature was climbing fast. By mile 40, it was brutal. It had already climbed to around 95 degrees in the shade, except there was no shade. I started consuming more fluids than planned. At every aid station, I grabbed extra bottles and poured water over my head and down my back. The relief lasted maybe 30 seconds before the sun baked me dry again.

Around mile 50, I noticed something concerning: Other riders were slowing dramatically. Some were pulled over on the side of the road, sitting in what little shade they could find. I remember riding by one guy who was lying flat on his back in the grass under a small tree. This wasn't normal race fatigue. This was heat taking people down.

I kept moving, kept drinking, kept dumping water over myself. It had to be over 100 degrees by this point. At the mile-60 aid station, the special-needs pickup, I stopped longer than planned. I grabbed my special-needs bag, refilled all my bottles, consumed a gel, drank a full bottle of sports drink, and just stood there for a moment trying to cool down.

A volunteer asked if I was okay. "Just hot," I said, which was the understatement of the day.

The second half was worse; the extreme heat made the rolling hills feel like mountains. The radiating sun drained energy I didn't have. My stomach started rebelling. I had consumed so much fluid and sugar that my gut couldn't process it all. I had to back off the nutrition, which meant I would pay for it later on the run. I pedaled through the final 20 miles on pure stubbornness, determined not to be one of the athletes loaded into the medical tent.

T2 was chaos of a different kind. Volunteers were everywhere with towels, ice, and water. Other athletes looked destroyed, faces red, movements slow, eyes unfocused. I grabbed my run gear bag and sat down to change shoes. That's when I realized how much the heat had taken out of me. My hands shook. My legs barely functioned. I felt dizzy just sitting there.

But I laced up my running shoes, grabbed my race belt and hat, and walked out into the late-afternoon heat for the marathon.

The first steps felt terrible. Like running through molasses. Like my legs belonged to someone else. The marathon course wound through downtown Louisville, two loops through neighborhoods, along the waterfront, past Churchill Downs. Under normal conditions it would be a beautiful run, but these were not normal conditions.

I made it maybe 2 miles before I had to adopt a run-walk strategy. Run to the next aid station. Walk through it. Consume everything available. Try to run to the next one.

At every aid station, I filled cups with ice and dumped them down my tri suit. I grabbed cold sponges and draped them over my neck. I consumed water, electrolytes, chicken broth, whatever they offered. And then around mile 6, I stopped sweating. That's when I knew I was in real danger. When your body stops sweating in 100-degree heat, it means you're severely dehydrated and could potentially be approaching heatstroke.

I tried to take in more liquids, but my stomach was done. The rest of the marathon was pure survival. I wasn't racing anymore. I was just trying to finish before my body shut down completely.

The course passed the medical tent multiple times, and each time I saw more athletes on cots with IV lines in their arms. The medical staff was overwhelmed with heat casualties. I heard later that more than 50 athletes were treated for severe dehydration that day, and tragically, one athlete had died during the swim portion.

Andrea found me around mile 15. Seeing her gave me a surge of energy, but it faded quickly. The heat was relentless. Mile 18. Mile 20. Mile 22. I kept moving, one foot in front of the other, telling myself that every step forward was one step closer to done.

Finally, around mile 24, I heard the announcer in the distance. The finish line was close.

I tried to run the final 2 miles but could only manage intervals: run 30 seconds, walk a minute, repeat. But I was moving toward the finish, and that's what mattered. The finish chute appeared, lined with spectators cheering. The lights, the noise, the announcer calling names, it all pulled me forward.

"Jason Millsaps, from Athens, Georgia . . . YOU ARE AN IRONMAN!"

Official time: 14:42:41.

Almost an hour slower than Arizona, but honestly, I was just grateful to be alive. A volunteer met up with me at the finish line, asked if I was okay, put a medal around my neck, and handed me bottles of water. I drank them both immediately.

The Aftermath

I then found Andrea, and she could see at once that I was struggling. "We need to get you sitting down," she said. We walked to the food tent, where I tried to eat but couldn't. I just kept drinking water, trying to rehydrate.

Then I looked at Andrea. I could tell she wasn't her cheerful self, especially after a race. She looked at me and reluctantly said, "I don't feel good."

Before I could respond, she sat down on the curb, then lay down on the sidewalk. Right there, in the middle of the finisher area, my wife was lying on the ground. I was thinking, *Shouldn't I be the one lying on the sidewalk?*

"I'm dizzy," she said. "I think I'm dehydrated."

Of course she was. She had spent the entire day in the heat, tracking me, running between spectator spots. Spectators don't get aid stations. They don't get volunteers checking on them. She had pushed herself to the limit supporting me, and now she was paying for it.

I couldn't even bend over to help her properly. My back was locked up from more than 14 hours of racing. So there we were, me barely able to move, her lying on the sidewalk, both of us completely spent. I thought our kids were supposed to take care of us when we turned old. Too bad our boys were staying with my parents during this race. We could've used them right then.

A volunteer brought Andrea water and helped her sit up. After about 10 minutes, she felt stable enough to walk. We made it back to the hotel, where Andrea spent the night throwing up from heat exhaustion and dehydration.

What a glamorous hobby I had chosen.

The Lessons

Louisville taught me things Arizona hadn't, like, conditions matter. You can train perfectly and still have a slow race if the weather doesn't cooperate. Sometimes survival is success. It also taught me to respect the heat. I had underestimated how oppressive heat would impact performance. Arizona had been warm, but Louisville was another level entirely. And most importantly, it taught me that spectators sacrifice too. Andrea's heat exhaustion (which was very serious at the time) reminded me that this wasn't just my race. She endured the same conditions I did, just without aid stations or medical support. The people who support you are running their own IRONMAN race. Every race following that, I think Andrea drank at least as much fluid as I consumed for each race.

Texas Awaits

December 2014 brought another change. Bell Shoals Church extended me the offer to be their Lead Worship Pastor, so we moved to Tampa, Florida. One advantage of moving to Florida was that I could train outdoors year-round without the cold.

Nine months after Louisville, I stood at another starting line. IRONMAN Texas in May 2015 arrived with the confidence that comes from experience. I'd completed two full IRONMAN races now. I knew the drill. I understood more about pacing, nutrition, and mental management. And this time, Scott was racing with me. After completing IRONMAN Arizona with me, his ninth IRONMAN race finish, he had decided to race Texas alongside me, attempting number 10. Having my coach on the course felt reassuring, like having a guide who knew exactly what to expect.

Arrival in Houston

Andrea and I flew into Houston on Thursday. The Woodlands is a nice community north of the city that transformed into a race venue for the weekend. Friday's practice swim was in a murky lake with a canal system, brown, warm, smelling of fish and algae. Nothing remarkable. The weather forecast called for possible rain but nothing severe.

Race Day

Saturday morning, race day, arrived at 4 a.m. with my standard prerace routine. It was already humid, classic Texas spring weather. Rain had fallen overnight, turning parts of the transition area into mud pits.

The swim was a little more crazy than Arizona or Louisville. The course made several turns around a lake and then went through a narrow canal that funneled 2,000 athletes together, creating a washing-machine effect of flailing arms and kicking legs. This wasn't swimming, it was aquatic combat.

I climbed out of the water and checked my watch: 1 hour, 55 minutes. That was nearly 35 minutes slower than my previous IRONMAN swims. Thirty-five minutes lost before the race even really started.

Transition 1 was literally a mud pit. My feet were muddy, my bike tires were muddy, everything was muddy. I actually had to carry my bike over my shoulder out of transition to where we mounted the bikes. But once on the road, I felt great. My nutrition plan was dialed in. I was disciplined and felt in control.

Then came mile 60.

The famous Texas wind that every veteran warns you about arrived with fury. What had been a gentle breeze became a sustained headwind that felt like pedaling through concrete. I watched my speed drop from 18 mph to 12 mph to 8 mph, all while maintaining the same effort. I was working as hard as I had been working uphill, but the road was flat.

Around me, other cyclists looked equally frustrated.

"Are your splits off?" someone shouted.

"Yeah! Are we even moving?"

We were, but barely.

The wind was so strong that descents felt like climbs. At one point, I was pedaling downhill, actually descending, and barely maintaining 10 to 12 mph. That's when I realized this day was going to be much harder than I had planned.

Suddenly, people were talking about cutoff times. That was the first moment fear crept in. I might not make it. IRONMAN races have strict cutoffs. You must complete the swim by a certain time, the bike by a certain time, and the full race by 17 hours from the start. Miss any cutoff and you're pulled from the course, a DNF (did not finish), regardless of how hard you've worked.

I had never worried about cutoffs before. Actually, I really hadn't given them much thought. But with the slow swim and now this brutal wind, the math was getting tight. I made the decision to abandon my careful pacing plan and push harder on the bike. I needed to bank time for what I knew would be a difficult run. I broke from my pace plan and started hammering. My stomach cramped. My nutrition slipped. The whole vibe turned from "race" to "survival."

I rolled into transition with 27 minutes to spare.

Bike time: 8:03:30.

Ugly. But I was still alive. I was still in the race.

Inside the changing tent, the crowd had thinned. I grabbed some ice water, changed socks, and put on my running shoes. The blister on my foot was already throbbing, but I jogged out, determined to run the marathon. I lasted 7 miles. By mile 8, my head was pounding, a sign of dehydration. My foot felt like it had a golf ball taped to the bottom. Every step was agony. I started walking. Aid stations became havens. Electrolyte drinks, chicken broth, chips, cookies, bananas, I tried everything. I just needed to keep moving. Around mile 10, I saw Andrea on the side of the course. She was cheering, but I could see something was off. Her expression was different.

I slowed down as I approached her.

"Scott didn't make it," she said. "He got pulled. He missed the bike cutoff."

I stopped completely. "What?!"

"He missed the cutoff by only a few minutes. They pulled him from the race."

I couldn't believe it. Scott. My coach. The man who had done 9 IRONMAN races, going for number 10. The person who'd taught me everything I knew about this sport. Pulled from the race. I knew the bike had been brutal. The wind had destroyed everyone out there. But it had never crossed my mind that one of us would have a DNF. That Scott, experienced, prepared, disciplined Scott, wouldn't make it.

"Are you okay?" Andrea asked, seeing the shock on my face.

"Yeah, I just . . . I can't believe it."

"He wants you to finish," she said. "Keep going."

I nodded, still processing. Part of me felt guilty, as if I should have been the one who didn't make it, not him. He was the experienced one. I was just the guy who could barely swim 37 yards three years ago.

But I was still in the race. And I had to finish it.

I hated this for Scott. Really hated it. But I started moving again, one painful step at a time. If Texas could take down a nine-time IRONMAN finisher, it could take down anyone. The fact that I was still out there, still moving forward, felt like borrowed time. Every mile from that point forward, I thought about Scott standing in transition, watching his race end after 112 brutal miles.

I was going to finish this. Not just for me, but for both of us.

I calculated my pace. If I walked 14-minute miles, I would finish with a 30-minute cushion. Not glamorous. Not my initial plan. But doable.

Then the course surprised me with stairs.

Yes. Stairs. During an IRONMAN marathon.

A construction detour forced all athletes to descend a short staircase on each loop, twice in total. By the second lap, my legs were Jell-O. The descent was actually comical, watching exhausted athletes grunt and hobble down stairs.

Somewhere around mile 23, I heard a volunteer yell, "You're gonna make it!"

And for the first time that day, I believed it.

I rounded the final corner and saw the green tape: FINISH THIS WAY.

I started running—okay, moving slightly faster. I high-fived strangers. I heard the crowd. Then I heard the Voice of IRONMAN, Mike Reilly, say, "From Tampa, Florida . . .

"Hey, Jason Millsaps, this crowd has something to say to you . . . YOU. ARE. AN. IRONMAN!"

The whole crowd was yelling for me.

Official time: 16:28:30.

My slowest IRONMAN race by far. Nearly three hours slower than Arizona.

The Reflection

Andrea met me in the finisher area, and I could see the relief in her eyes. She had been tracking both of us all day. My friends and family had been texting Andrea all day asking if something was wrong, since . . . I was taking forever to finish.

"Wow. That was rough," I said, still catching my breath.

"But you finished," she said.

"I still can't believe Scott didn't make it."

"I know. He's disappointed, but he's okay. He's proud of you."

Later that evening, I found Scott in the hotel lobby. He looked tired but composed.

"Hey, Coach," I said, not sure what else to say.

"Congrats on finishing," he said, and he meant it. "That was a brutal day out there."

"I heard about the cutoff. I'm so sorry."

He shrugged. "That's racing. Some days everything clicks. Some days it doesn't. Today wasn't my day."

"You've finished nine of these. I never thought—"

"Neither did I," he interrupted with a slight smile. "But that's IRONMAN. It doesn't matter how many you've done before. Each race is its own challenge. Texas won today. At least for me."

There was a pause, then he said, "But you gutted it out. You finished when everything went wrong. That's what I've been trying to teach you—not how to have a perfect race, but how to finish an imperfect one. You did that."

"Thanks for everything, Scott. For believing in me."

"Always. Now get some rest. We've got more races ahead of us."

I walked away thinking about what he'd said: *Texas won today. At least for me.*

But it hadn't won against both of us. And that mattered.

The Wisdom

Louisville and Texas weren't about my times or achieving personal records. They were about finishing when everything goes wrong. When conditions turn against you. When your body says no and your plan falls apart.

Even the experienced have bad days. Scott had completed nine IRONMAN races before Texas. He knew how to pace, how to fuel, how to manage the mental game. But conditions don't care about your experience or your credentials. When I learned he had been pulled from the race, missing the bike cutoff by seriously less than five minutes, I didn't believe it. It had never crossed my mind that one of us would DNF, and certainly not him. But Texas was a humbling reminder that some days, the course wins. Even against the best.

Finding out that Scott had been pulled from the race, even though I only learned about it during my run, was one of the hardest moments of the day. But it also taught me something: Failure doesn't erase your other accomplishments. Scott was still a nine-time IRONMAN finisher. One DNF didn't change that. And his disappointment made my finish feel even more meaningful. I wasn't just finishing for me anymore. I was finishing for both of us.

The Medals

The medals from Louisville and Texas now hang on the wall with my other IRONMAN race medals, but they carry different weights. They're not medals for fast races; they're medals for not quitting when quitting looked appealing. And sometimes that's the most important finish of all.

The Questions

How do you define success when conditions make your original goals impossible?

What do you do when the race becomes about survival instead of competition?

And what do you learn when someone you respect—someone more experienced than you—falls short while you somehow make it through?

Sometimes the races that break you are the ones that prove you won't stay broken.

The Body Breaks

"The greatest glory in living lies not in never falling, but in rising every time we fall."
—NELSON MANDELA

February 2022. Ten years after I could barely swim 37 yards. Twelve IRONMAN race finishes under my belt:

- 2013 IRONMAN Arizona
- 2014 IRONMAN Louisville, KY
- 2015 IRONMAN Texas (The Woodlands)
- 2016 IRONMAN Florida (Panama City, FL)
- 2017 IRONMAN Florida (Panama City, FL)
- 2018 IRONMAN Texas (The Woodlands)
- 2018 IRONMAN Florida (Panama City, FL)
- 2018 IRONMAN Chattanooga, TN
- 2019 IRONMAN Texas (The Woodlands)
- 2019 IRONMAN Florida (Haines City, FL)
- 2021 IRONMAN Lake Placid, NY
- 2021 IRONMAN Arizona

Twelve times I had pushed my body through 2.4 miles of swimming, 112 miles of biking, and 26.2 miles of running. Twelve times I had crossed the finish line victorious. Twelve times I had proved that ordinary people can do extraordinary things. But the body keeps score. And in February 2022, the bill came due.

The Shift

I was on the treadmill at the YMCA, grinding through a routine nine-mile run. Nothing special, just another weekday workout in preparation for IRONMAN Texas in April, about 10 weeks away. Around mile seven, I felt something shift in my lower back. Not pain exactly. More like a sensation that something had gone wrong. Like a door closing that shouldn't close. Or a piece sliding out of place. I finished the run, because that's what you do when you've completed 12 IRONMAN races—you ignore warning signs and push through discomfort. (That's not advice, by the way.) I had built a decade-long career on ignoring my body's protests.

I drove home, showered, and called my chiropractor. He had been adjusting me for years, working through the normal aches and pains that come with endurance training.

"Can you get me in today?" I asked.

"Sure. Come by this afternoon."

He adjusted me, told me to ice it, and sent me home. No big deal. I had dealt with minor back issues before, so this felt like my normal routine.

The Morning After

The next morning, I could barely get out of bed. Not in the "I'm sore and tired" way. In the "something is seriously wrong" way. I managed to get up slowly but immediately collapsed back onto the mattress, face down. I tried to roll to my side and couldn't. Every movement sent shooting pain down both legs, the kind of pain that makes you gasp, that steals your breath, that makes you wonder if something is broken.

Andrea walked into the room and asked what I was doing.

"I can't get up," I said.

"What do you mean you can't get up?"

"I mean I literally cannot move. Something's really wrong."

"We need to get you to the doctor," she said.

"I can't sit in a car. I can't even stand."

"Then we're calling an ambulance."

"No," I said. Too expensive. Too dramatic. "Just help me figure out how to get back to the chiropractor."

Somehow, I don't remember exactly how, I was able to get into Andrea's SUV.

Andrea had to take our boys to school, but after sitting for just 10 seconds, I couldn't sit any longer in the car. I opened the car door and got out. I just knelt down and then lay down on the concrete floor as Andrea left to take the boys to school. She shut the garage door so our neighbors wouldn't think I had died, and I just lay there in the middle of the garage, now in complete darkness.

Andrea came back to get me, and I finally managed to sit in the car long enough for her to drive me to the chiropractor. He took one look at me trying to walk and said, "You're going straight to the ER." The diagnosis: ruptured discs at L5 and S1. The ER doctor referred me to a neurosurgeon.

IRONMAN Texas in 10 weeks? Not happening.

The Scans

The ER doctor ordered scans immediately. MRI, X-rays, the full workup. When he came back with the results, his expression told me everything before he said a word. "You have a ruptured disc at L5 and S1 and two herniated discs above it," he said, pulling up the images on the computer. "See here? The disc material is herniated and pressing directly on your nerve roots. That's why you're experiencing the radiating pain down both legs."

I stared at the images. Even I could see the problem: bulging disc material where there should have been space.

"What does this mean?" Andrea asked.

"He needs to see a neurosurgeon next week," the doctor said.

"What about the IRONMAN race in April?" I asked.

The doctor looked at me like I had suggested running a marathon on a broken leg.

"You need to focus on being able to walk without pain first," he said.

Second Opinion

I saw the first neurosurgeon, who quickly recommended surgery, but I wanted to get a second opinion. My parents connected me with a neurosurgeon friend of theirs who practiced in Fort Myers, Dr. Michael Fromke. The earliest appointment was in two days, which felt like an eternity when every movement hurt.

Those two days were among the worst of my life. I couldn't sit. Couldn't stand for more than a few minutes. Couldn't lie down comfortably. Sleep was impossible. I spent most of the time lying on the couch, trying different positions, searching for any arrangement of my body that didn't trigger the electric pain down my legs.

Andrea had to help me with everything. Getting dressed. Getting to the bathroom. Moving from room to room. I quickly went from someone who could swim 2.4 miles, bike 112 miles, and run a marathon in a single day to someone who couldn't put on his own socks.

The humiliation was almost worse than the pain.

What They Saw

Jonathan and Jaden saw their dad, the guy who had completed 12 IRONMAN races, who woke up at 4:30 a.m. to train, who'd taught them that you don't quit when things get hard, lying on the floor, unable to function.

"Is Dad going to be okay?" I heard Jaden ask Andrea one evening.

"Yes," she said with more confidence than I felt. "He just needs to get his back fixed."

The Appointment

The two-hour drive to Fort Myers was anything but comfortable. Andrea drove while I laid my seat back just right trying to alleviate the pain. Dr. Fromke's office was professional, calm, the kind of place that regularly treats serious spinal injuries. Dr. Fromke reviewed my scans and examination results, then explained what was happening.

"You have significant disc herniations at L5–S1," he said, using his pen to point at the images on his computer screen. "The disc material is compressing your nerve roots, which is why you're experiencing pain, numbness, and weakness in both legs."

"Can you fix it?" I asked.

"We can try conservative treatment first—rest, anti-inflammatories, physical therapy. Sometimes these herniations will reduce on their own over time."

"And if they don't?"

"Then we consider a microdiscectomy, which is minimally invasive surgery to remove the herniated portion of the disc that's pressing on your nerves."

Andrea spoke up. "What's the recovery time for surgery?"

"Eight to 12 weeks, typically. With you being in good shape, your body should respond well. Let's try conservative treatment for a few weeks," he said. "See if rest and therapy help. If you're not improving, we'll schedule surgery."

Conservative Treatment

The next four weeks were horrible. I couldn't train. Couldn't swim, couldn't bike, couldn't run. I could barely walk around the block without my legs going numb. I lead worship every Sunday, and I couldn't even stand to do that. We moved a piano out on the stage, and I led from there for the next several weeks.

Physical therapy twice a week consisted of stretches and exercises that felt impossibly hard. Things like lying on my back and lifting one leg a few inches off the table, movements that should have been trivial but left me gasping in pain.

The therapist was patient, encouraging. "You're doing great. This is progress."

It didn't feel like progress. It felt like failure.

Every morning, I would wake up hoping the pain would be better. And every morning, it was the same. Sharp, electric, painful.

I wasn't just in physical pain; I started to feel emotional pain. Not only was I a worship pastor, but people knew me as an IRONMAN finisher. For the past 10 years I had been known as an endurance athlete. Someone who could push through anything. Someone who didn't quit. Now I couldn't even walk to the mailbox without stopping to rest.

Maybe this was an opportunity to figure out who I was without triathlon racing in my life.

The Decision

Four weeks into conservative treatment, nothing had improved. If anything, the pain was worse. Dr. Fromke ordered new scans. The results were clear: The herniation hadn't reduced. Surgery was the next step. We scheduled the microdiscectomy for May 2, 2022.

I had already deferred my Texas race entry to IRONMAN Waco, which was scheduled in October. This gave me more time to take care of my back.

I sent a text to Scott: *Can't race Texas. Having back surgery. Will keep you posted on recovery.*

His response came within minutes: *Take care of yourself. The races will always be there. Your health comes first.*

The night before surgery, I couldn't sleep. Not from fear of the surgery itself—I trusted Dr. Fromke—but from fear of what came after.

What if I never raced again?

What if this was the end?

What if 10 years of building myself into an endurance athlete ended on an operating table in Fort Myers?

Andrea found me awake at 2 a.m., staring at the ceiling.

"Can't sleep?" she asked.

"Just thinking."

"About?"

"What if I can't come back from this?"

She was quiet for a moment. "Then you'll find something else. But you've come back from everything else. You are too strong-willed. You'll come back from this too."

"I sure hope so," I said.

"You will. I know you. You're stubborn. You don't quit. Even when you probably should."

That got a small smile out of me.

"Tomorrow, they fix what's broken," she said. "And then we start rebuilding. One day at a time. Just like you did when you could only swim 37 yards."

Surgery Day

Surgery day arrived early. We checked in at 5 a.m. The pre-op routine was normal—IV line, hospital gown, endless questions about allergies and medical history.

Dr. Fromke came by before they wheeled me to the operating room.

"How are you feeling?" he asked.

"Let's get this thing done."

"We're going to take good care of you. The surgery should take a couple of hours. We'll remove the herniated disc material, decompress the nerve roots, and you should experience immediate pain relief."

Andrea gave me a kiss and told me she loved me, and then they wheeled me down the hallway toward the operating room.

Then the doors closed, and I was alone with the surgical team.

The anesthesiologist placed the mask over my face. "Count backward from 10."

"Ten . . . nine . . . eight . . ."

And then nothing.

Recovery

I woke up in recovery with a dry throat and a foggy mind. A nurse was checking my vitals.

"Jason? Jason?" in a soft voice.

"Yeah."

"Surgery went well. Dr. Fromke will be by to talk to you shortly. How's your pain?"

I did a mental inventory. The sharp, electric pain down my legs, the pain that had defined the past six weeks, was gone.

"It's . . . gone," I said, shocked.

"That's great news. That means we got good decompression."

Dr. Fromke appeared a few minutes later, still in his surgical scrubs.

"Everything went well," he said. "We removed the herniated disc material and cleaned up the area. Your nerve roots should have plenty of space now.

"No bending, lifting, or twisting for six weeks. We'll start physical therapy soon. After six weeks, we'll reassess and talk about gradually returning to activity."

"Do you think I can race Waco in October?"

"If you follow the recovery protocol and listen to your body, yes. But first things first. Let's recover."

I nodded, but inside I was already planning my comeback.

The first few days after surgery were brutal. Not only was the pain bad, every slight movement terrified me. What if I bent wrong and re-herniated the disc? What if I twisted and undid everything the surgery had fixed? What if I sneezed and my back exploded?

Andrea had to help me with everything. Getting dressed, getting to the bathroom, moving from bed to couch. I had gone from needing help because of the herniation to needing help because I was terrified of damaging the surgical repair.

"You have to move," Andrea said gently on day three. "The doctor said walking is good for recovery."

"What if something goes wrong?"

"Then we deal with it. But you can't just lie here. You'll make it worse."

She was right. I knew she was right. But knowing and doing were different things.

That afternoon, I took my walker outside and walked down the sidewalk in front of our house. Maybe 50 yards total. It took 15 minutes and left me exhausted. But I moved. The next day, we walked to the neighbor's driveway. Then to the end of the street. Then around the block.

I started timing my walks on my Garmin, the same watch that had tracked thousands of training miles. When I started, I was doing 45-minute miles. Now it was tracking 20-minute miles around my neighborhood. But they were miles. And miles were progress.

Four weeks post-surgery, I asked Dr. Fromke the question that had been consuming me: "Can I swim?"

He considered. "Yes. Swimming should be fine. The water supports your body weight and reduces stress on your spine. Start with easy laps, no flip turns, no aggressive kicking. Just smooth, controlled swimming."

That afternoon, I went to the pool for the first time since March.

Standing at the edge, I felt both excitement and fear. What if it hurt? What if I had lost everything I had built over 10 years?

I slipped into the water and started swimming.

Slow, controlled freestyle. No racing. No pushing. No twisting. Just moving through the water.

One lap. Two laps. Three.

My stroke was rusty, my conditioning was shot, but I was swimming. I was swimming.

When I climbed out after 10 lengths of the pool, just 250 yards, I was exhausted, but relieved.

I texted Andrea from the parking lot. "I swam. I actually swam."

"How'd it feel?"

"Really good."

"I'm proud of you."

I then started physical therapy. The therapist was patient and knowledgeable. "We're going to rebuild your core strength and teach your body to move properly again. We're starting from scratch."

The exercises were humbling. Things like lying on my back and lifting one knee toward my chest. Or standing and marching in place. Or being on all fours and trying to stretch my leg straight back.

These weren't IRONMAN exercises. These were "learning to be a functional human" exercises. But I did them religiously. Twice a week at the clinic, twice a week at home. I treated physical therapy with the same discipline I applied to IRONMAN training.

By week six, the physical therapist introduced the antigravity treadmill—a machine that uses air pressure to reduce your body weight. She set it to 50 percent of my body weight and had me walk for 10 minutes.

It felt like flying. Like my body remembered how to move without pain.

"Can I run?" I asked.

"Not yet. Walking only for now. We'll gradually add running when your body is ready."

I had my six-week follow-up appointment with Dr. Fromke.

"How are you feeling?" he asked.

"Better. The nerve pain is gone. I'm walking without issues. I've been swimming."

"That's great progress. Let's check your range of motion."

He had me bend, twist, and stretch through various movements. Everything felt stable.

"You're healing well," he said. "You can start gradually increasing activity."

"What about our trip to Hawaii? What about racing?"

"You are clear to fly to Hawaii for your anniversary trip, but no cliff diving or anything crazy." He laughed, but was serious. "The racing will come. Let's get through the next few weeks and build back your base fitness. If everything stays stable, you should be good to do IRONMAN Waco in the fall."

Hawaii

July 2022. Andrea and I flew to Hawaii for our 20th-anniversary trip. Ten weeks post-surgery, I was walking pain-free, swimming regularly, and cautiously optimistic about my future. When we came back up to the room from the beach in Honolulu, I saw that I had an email from IRONMAN.

Subject: IRONMAN Legacy Program—2023 World Championship Assignment

I stared at the subject line, almost afraid to open it.

The Legacy Program. I had applied two years earlier, knowing I needed at least 12 IRONMAN finishes to be eligible. I had hit 12 just before the surgery.

I opened the email.

We are pleased to inform you that you are hereby assigned to participate in the 2023 IRONMAN World Championship through the Legacy Program.

I read it three times to make sure I wasn't misunderstanding.

I was in. I was going to Kona.

"Andrea," I said, my voice shaking slightly.

"What?"

I handed her the phone.

She read the email, then looked at me with a mixture of excitement and concern. "This is what you've wanted for 10 years."

"I know!"

"Can you do it? After the surgery?"

"You know I can!"

To maintain Legacy eligibility, I needed to complete at least one full IRONMAN race in 2022. With my surgery in May and recovery taking months, I had one option: IRONMAN Waco in October.

Five months post-surgery. Barely enough time to rebuild. But if I didn't race, I could lose my Kona slot.

The next three months were a careful balance between rebuilding and not rushing.

I swam three times a week. Biked on my indoor trainer, sitting up more than getting in aero position, trying to avoid extra stress on my back. Walked a lot. Listening obsessively to every sensation in my lower back and legs.

Physical therapy continued twice a week. The therapist pushed me to rebuild core strength, the foundation that would protect my spine during long races, and I would eventually start running on the antigravity treadmill, decreasing the weight each week. Everyone knew I was building to make it to IRONMAN Waco.

Andrea watched me closely. "How are you feeling? Really?"

"Scared," I admitted. "Every time I have a twinge or a weird sensation, I think I've re-herniated the disc. But also . . . determined. I'm not done yet."

IRONMAN Waco

October 2022. IRONMAN Waco. Five months post-surgery. Standing at the starting line, I felt different than at any other race. This wasn't about time or competition. This was about proving I could still do this. That surgery hadn't ended my racing career.

The swim and bike went fine; not fast, not impressive, but functional. I wasn't trying to break any records. I just wanted to finish this race healthy. The marathon was something I never want to experience again, but not because of my back. Just from being undertrained and pushing a body that wasn't quite ready. I walked the entire 26.2 miles. Which might actually be harder than running. Official time: 16:12:10.

One of my slowest IRONMAN races ever. But it didn't matter. What mattered was that my back was still feeling better and I had validated my Legacy status for 2022. Kona 2023 was still on track.

Standing at that finish line in Waco, medal around my neck and body completely spent, I thought about the journey from lying on my garage floor to now completing 140.6 miles. Surgery had taught me something crucial: Setbacks don't have to be endings. They can be detours. Sometimes the body says no, and you have to listen. But "no" doesn't always mean "never." Sometimes it just means "not yet." The road to Kona was longer than I had planned. But I was still on it.

The Change

In late November 2022, another email from IRONMAN arrived.

Due to logistical considerations, the 2023 IRONMAN World Championship will be split by gender. Women will race in Kona, Hawaii, in October 2023. Men will race in Nice, France, in September 2023.

I read it twice, trying to process what this meant.

Nice was an incredible opportunity, racing the World Championship on roads used by the Tour de France. But it wasn't what I had been chasing for over a decade. It wasn't Kona. The email offered a choice: Race Nice in 2023, or defer to Kona 2024. I chose Kona. Which meant waiting another year. Another full season. Another year of wondering if my surgically repaired back would hold up. And to stay eligible for the Legacy Program, I would need to complete another full IRONMAN race in 2023.

The finish line I'd been chasing had moved farther away, but at least I could still see it.

The Questions

What setback in your life has felt like an ending but might actually be a detour?

How do you respond when your body, your circumstances, or your limitations tell you to stop?

Do you see setbacks as failures, or as opportunities to rebuild stronger foundations?

Often the distance between giving up and pushing through comes down to one question: Are you willing to start over at a slower pace if that's what it takes to keep moving forward?

10

Stubborn in the Right Direction

*"Everybody has a plan until
they get punched in the mouth."*
—MIKE TYSON

I had deferred Kona to 2024, which meant I had more time to train, recover, and prepare properly. That should have felt like plenty of time. It should have been a gift, space to rebuild wisely instead of rushing. But to stay eligible for the Legacy Program, I again needed to complete one full IRONMAN race in 2023. One race to keep my Kona slot alive.

I registered for IRONMAN Tulsa, happening in May 2023, giving myself a spring race to validate my Legacy status while building toward Kona the following year. Training through the winter of 2022–2023 felt good initially. I was stronger than I had been post-surgery, more confident, pushing harder. My back seemed fine. The microdiscectomy had worked. I was healed. Or so I thought.

Spring Break

In March 2023, our family took a spring break vacation to Washington, DC. We had been planning the trip for months; museums, monuments, historical sites. Quality time with Andrea and the boys exploring the nation's capital.

The first day, we walked the National Mall, visiting the Lincoln Memorial, the Washington Monument, the World War II Memorial. Miles of walking on concrete paths under a warm spring sun.

Around lunchtime, I had to sit down.

"You okay?" Andrea asked.

"Yeah, just tired."

But it wasn't normal tired. My legs ached in ways that felt disturbingly familiar. Not muscle soreness from walking, but nerve pain shooting down both legs, the same sensation I had felt before the first surgery.

I rested for a few minutes, stood up, and we continued. Fifteen minutes later, I had to sit again.

This pattern repeated all afternoon. Walk for 10 or 15 minutes, then sit down to rest, trying to ignore the burning sensation running from my lower back down both legs.

"Dad, why do we keep stopping?" my youngest asked.

"Because I'm an old man," I said, which wasn't technically a lie.

Andrea gave me a look that said she knew something was wrong.

That evening, back at the hotel, she asked directly: "Is it your back?"

"I don't know. Maybe from all the walking."

"Jason."

"I'm fine," I said, which was my automatic response even when I wasn't fine.

But I wasn't fine, and we both knew it.

The next day, we visited the Smithsonian museums. More walking. More frequent stops. By day three, every 15 minutes I had to find a bench, a wall, anything to take pressure off my back and let the nerve pain subside. The boys were patient, but I could see their confusion. Why couldn't Dad walk like a normal person? Why were we spending half our vacation sitting?

Andrea told me, "You need to call your doctor."

"It's probably from all the activity. I'll rest this week and it'll be fine."

"Jason, you can barely walk for more than 10 minutes. That's not normal."

She was right. But acknowledging it meant facing something I didn't want to face: the possibility that my back surgery hadn't fixed the problem, that something was still wrong, that my IRONMAN dreams might be over.

The Avoidance

Back home in Florida, I tried to resume training. But the symptoms persisted. Pain when walking or running, but oddly, nothing when I swam or biked. I could ride my bike for two hours without issue, but a 30-minute walk would leave me in agony.

I tried to convince myself it was temporary. A flare-up. It would resolve with rest and stretching. I tried to avoid messaging Dr. Fromke, hoping the problem would disappear on its own. It didn't. I finally messaged him hoping he would tell me this was normal in the healing process. He didn't say that. He immediately responded and told me to come see him. They scheduled me for the following week.

The Diagnosis

The two-hour drive to Fort Myers with Andrea felt heavier this time. We had been here before, a year ago; same route, same surgeon, same hope that he could fix what was broken. But this time felt different. This time, I knew it might not be a simple fix.

The surgeon reviewed my symptoms and ordered new MRI scans.

We sat in his office while he pulled up the MRI images on his computer. Even I could see the problem, or rather, the absence. Where there should have been a disc cushioning my vertebrae, there was nothing. Bone touching bone.

"With all the training and racing you've done since the microdiscectomy," he said, "your disc is completely gone now. Bone-on-bone contact. The previous surgery removed the herniated portion, but you've done a great job pounding away what remained."

The words hung in the air.

"It's not going to get better on its own," he continued. "You need spinal fusion surgery."

I had researched spinal fusion after the first surgery, hoping I would never need it. Now here we were.

He explained the procedure in detail: He would access my spine through the front of my abdomen first, then flip me over to work from the back. A cage would be placed between L5 and S1, secured with rods and screws to stabilize the damaged area. Recovery would be longer, 6 to 7 months before I could resume serious training and 12 months for a full recovery.

"Can I still race?" I asked, which was probably the wrong first question but the only one that mattered to me in that moment.

"Race when?"

"IRONMAN Tulsa. It's in six weeks."

He looked at me like I had suggested climbing Everest in flip-flops.

"You've already done the damage. The disc is already gone," he said carefully. "Racing won't do further damage because there's nothing left to damage. If you can tolerate the pain, you could finish."

Andrea spoke up. "And if he doesn't race Tulsa? If he has surgery now?"

"Then we schedule it immediately. He recovers properly. And he should be cleared to train again by late fall, which gives him plenty of time to prepare for Kona in October 2024."

The math was simple. Skip Tulsa, have surgery now, recover properly, train for Kona. The smart choice was obvious.

Except it wasn't that simple.

I knew I needed the surgery, and I wanted to remain eligible for the Legacy program. I looked at Andrea, and she already knew what I would choose.

I told the surgeon, "Let's schedule the surgery for the week after Tulsa."

That night, it was hard to sleep.

The surgeon had been clear: Racing Tulsa wouldn't cause additional damage. The disc was gone. I would be racing in pain, which I had done before. Every IRONMAN race involved pain. This would just be . . . more pain.

But was I chasing a dream or running from the reality that maybe my body was telling me to stop?

I thought about my sons. What example was I setting? That you should push through pain no matter what? That goals matter more than health? That stubbornness is the same as perseverance?

Or was I teaching them that you don't give up when things get hard? That setbacks are temporary? That you honor your commitments even when they're difficult?

I honestly didn't know anymore.

Training for Tulsa with a destroyed disc was probably not the smartest thing I've done, but I knew I couldn't make it any worse. Every run was painful. Every walk reminded me something was seriously wrong. But I did what I could. I swam regularly, biked when my back cooperated, and told myself this was just another challenge to overcome.

The boys knew something was wrong. They had seen me struggle in Washington, DC. They noticed I wasn't running as much.

"Dad, are you okay?" my oldest asked one evening.

"Yeah, buddy. Just some back issues."

"Are you still doing that race?"

"Yeah."

"Why? If your back hurts, why not skip it?"

Out of the mouths of teenagers.

"Because I set out to race Kona, and that's what I'm doing," I said. "And sometimes you have to keep going even when it's hard."

IRONMAN Tulsa

Race day in Tulsa arrived, and I lined up knowing full well what was waiting on the other side: major surgery, long recovery, uncertainty about whether I would ever be the same. But I also knew this was my last chance to keep my Kona dream alive.

The swim went fine. The bike was manageable, though my back ached more than usual. But the marathon was agony. Every step sent pain radiating down both legs. At each aid station, I filled a bag with ice and stuffed it down the back of my tri suit, letting it sit directly on my lower back. The cold numbed the pain enough for me to keep moving.

I ran when I could, walked when I had to. Somewhere around mile 15, I asked myself, *What am I doing? Why am I putting myself through this?* The answer came from a deeper place: *Because Kona. Because you've come too far to quit now. Because this pain is temporary, but giving up lasts forever.*

I crossed the finish line at 13:52:02.

IRONMAN race number 14.

One week later, Andrea and I drove back to Fort Myers for surgery.

The Questions

How do you know when perseverance becomes stubbornness?

When does pushing through pain become ignoring your body's warnings?

What's the difference between the discipline that builds character and the compulsion that breaks your body?

These are questions every high achiever must wrestle with. Because the same drive that accomplishes extraordinary things can also destroy you if you don't know when to stop and rebuild. Sometimes the bravest thing you can do isn't pushing through—it's choosing to heal properly, even when it means facing uncertainty about your future. I chose to push through. Some would call that courageous, and others would call it foolish. I'll let you decide.

12 Years to Kona

May 2023. One week after crossing the finish line in Tulsa, I was back on an operating table in Fort Myers for spinal fusion surgery. Recovery from spinal fusion is measured in months, not weeks. The surgeon had been clear: six to seven months before I could resume serious training. Twelve months for full recovery.

That timeline put me at late 2023 before I could properly prepare for Kona in October 2024. So I waited. And waiting, I learned, is its own kind of endurance event.

The first few weeks post-surgery were spent relearning basic movements. Walking without the walker became a milestone. Getting dressed without help felt like a victory. Taking a shower without Andrea's assistance was cause for celebration. Unlike after the first surgery, I didn't have formal physical therapy this time. The fusion was more invasive, and the recovery protocol was simpler: walk, move carefully, let the bone heal, and gradually increase activity as tolerated.

So I walked. Every day, timing myself on my Garmin like I timed marathon splits. The first walks were painfully slow. Shuffling around the block with my walker took 30 minutes. But each day brought improvement: seconds shaved off, then minutes. The data didn't lie. I was getting stronger.

I created my own recovery program based on what I had learned from the first surgery. The boys watched this slow progression with a mix of concern and curiosity.

"Dad, you used to run marathons," Jaden said one evening, watching me celebrate completing a one-mile walk. "And now you're excited about walking a mile?"

"That's right," I said. "Because three weeks ago, I couldn't walk to the mailbox. Progress is progress, no matter how small it looks."

Andrea reminded him, "Your dad just had major surgery. The fact that he's walking at all is amazing."

Around week four post-surgery, I was cleared to swim. I approached the pool cautiously, knowing that swimming involved twisting motions that could stress the fusion. I focused on smooth freestyle with minimal rotation, no flip turns, no aggressive kicking. Just moving through the water, reconnecting with the discipline that had started this whole journey 12 years ago.

For the first time since surgery, I felt like an athlete again instead of a patient. But I still couldn't run. Couldn't bike outdoors. Couldn't do any of the training that made me feel fully alive.

The Space

The forced slowdown created space I hadn't experienced in years, space to think about what came next. What if my body never fully recovered? What if Kona didn't happen? What if this was the end of my racing journey? I needed purpose beyond my own athletic goals.

During recovery, while scrolling through my phone, unable to train, unable to work normally, I came across information about triathlon coaching certifications. The idea had been growing in my mind since the first surgery. What would I do after racing? What if I could help others accomplish what Scott had helped me accomplish?

I registered for the USA Triathlon (USAT) Level 1 certification program, focusing on long-distance coaching. Then I added the TrainingPeaks Level 1 and then Level 2 certification for good measure.

If I couldn't train my own body properly right now, I could learn how to help others train theirs. Andrea found me one evening, laptop open, taking notes on exercise physiology.

"What are you working on?" she asked.

"Coaching certification. Learning about periodization, training adaptations, and how to design programs for different athlete types."

She smiled. "That's perfect for you."

"You think so?"

"Yeah. You already help others every day in your job. So, yes, adding coaching makes sense, and this will give you something to focus on besides your own recovery." She was right. The certifications gave me what surgery had taken away: forward momentum. Purpose. A reason to study and learn even when I couldn't train.

I would still wake up early before heading to the office, and instead of training, I would spend those hours watching training videos, reading coaching manuals, studying the science of endurance training. I took tests and absorbed everything I could about training methodology, nutrition strategies, injury prevention, and athlete psychology.

I thought about some of the mistakes I had made early in my racing career. Training too hard too soon. Ignoring warning signs. Racing through injuries. Treating my body as if it were indestructible. If I could help other athletes avoid those mistakes, maybe all my setbacks would serve a purpose beyond my own story.

The destroyed disc at L5–S1 wasn't bad luck. It was the cumulative result of 12 years of high-impact training, multiple IRONMAN races, and maybe a refusal to properly rest and recover.

Maybe I was starting to see the important part of rest, that rest is not weakness but is part of training. Taking care of yourself isn't selfish; it's necessary if you want to keep doing what you love.

Monitoring More Than Metrics

During those years of training and racing, I had to constantly monitor more than just my swim, bike, and run metrics. I had to monitor my soul.

In 2019, I spent a few days in Colorado with my good friend Lance Witt, a life coach and mentor to many. Lance taught me about "life buckets," the areas of life that must be regularly filled to stay replenished. He stood in front of me as I sat at a table, watching him draw one circle in the middle of a large sheet of paper. That circle represented me. Then he drew five circles surrounding the center circle. He asked me to start listing things that filled "my tank," and then to rate them red (empty), yellow (partial), or green (full).

My five buckets at the time:

1. Get away with Andrea three times a year—Red

2. Read one book per month—Yellow

3. Be engaged in my kids' activities—Yellow

4. Spend consistent time in personal worship—Yellow/Green

5. Do physical training four times a week—Green

Seeing it laid out, I realized I wasn't as balanced as I thought. If that had been my training log, I wouldn't be ready for a sprint triathlon, let alone a full IRONMAN race. My personal ambitions had slowly overshadowed my most important roles as a spiritual leader, husband, and father. I needed to realign.

My buckets have slightly adjusted over the years as the boys are getting older and activities change, but this self-check became a new rhythm. Just like I monitor fitness and fatigue during training, I began monitoring my soul and priorities the same way. Those five buckets became a mirror that didn't lie.

If you've never done this exercise, I encourage you to pause here. Draw your five replenishment buckets. Be honest. This kind of check-in is just as important as a training log review. You can't lead well, at home or at work, if your core buckets are empty. This is something I have to continue working on day after day.

As I headed into 2024 and the possibility of racing Kona, I knew that if I couldn't keep those buckets balanced, the race would mean nothing. Andrea wasn't going to let me forget it, and I'm grateful for that.

121 Tri Coaching

By late summer 2023, three months post-surgery, I had completed both coaching certifications. I was swimming regularly, walking several miles a day, and starting to add light stationary biking.

I decided to make coaching official. I built a website and created 121 Tri Coaching, named for one-on-one individualized coaching and Hebrews 12:1, the verse that had carried me through so many hard miles: *"Therefore, since we are surrounded by such a great cloud of witnesses, let us throw off everything that hinders and the sin that so easily entangles. And let us run with perseverance the race marked out for us."*

The name reflected both the personalized approach I wanted to take with athletes and the faith that had sustained me through this journey. I didn't know when I would start coaching, but I wanted to be ready. I created training plan templates, wrote athlete questionnaires, and developed intake processes.

Medical Clearance

October 2023, five months post-surgery, brought my follow-up appointment with Dr. Fromke. He reviewed my progress, checked my range of motion, and studied the latest scans showing the fusion solidifying.

"How are you feeling?" he asked.

"Good. Strong. Ready to start training for Kona 2024. I think."

He considered this carefully. "The fusion looks solid. Your mobility is good. You've been smart about the recovery process so far. I'm clearing you to start training again—but slowly and carefully. Build volume gradually. If you experience any nerve pain, numbness, or weakness, you stop immediately."

"I will."

I left that appointment with official clearance to train for Kona. Twelve months away. Time to prepare properly.

But I was nervous.

What if my back couldn't handle IRONMAN training? What if the fusion failed?

Training Begins

In November 2023, I officially began training for Kona. But this time, I wasn't just an athlete training for a race. I was now a coach who happened to be training for a race. I still used Scott to build my training plan and help serve as accountability for all my training sessions.

I also hired a professional sports nutritionist, Coach Elizabeth Inpyn, to help me with my post-surgery weight gain and muscle loss. I knew I needed expert guidance to optimize my nutrition for IRONMAN training. She helped me understand the relationship between protein intake and muscle recovery, the importance of adequate carbohydrates for endurance work, and how to fuel properly around long training sessions.

Rather than restrictive dieting, we focused on strategic fueling, eating enough to support the training load while gradually returning to race weight. Planning meals ahead, being intentional about nutrition timing, treating food as fuel rather than the enemy. The process was gradual and sustainable. My body responded to the combination of consistent training and proper nutrition.

But running still terrified me.

The memory of that treadmill run in March 2022 that led to the first surgery, feeling something shift in my back, still haunted me. And the gradual deterioration that led to the second surgery made me cautious about every step.

In February 2024, I finally laced up my running shoes and stepped outside for my first real run in nearly a year. I walked for five minutes to warm up, then jogged for 30 seconds.

Thirty seconds felt eternal. My back felt every impact. My fused spine felt stiff, unfamiliar. Everything in me wanted to stop.

But I didn't.

I walked for five more minutes, then jogged another 30 seconds. It was like Couch to 5K all over again. Starting from zero. Rebuilding from the foundation up.

Over the next weeks, 30 seconds became a minute. One minute became two. Two minutes became five.

By March 2024, I was officially in full IRONMAN training mode. Scott sent me a detailed plan, modified for my post-surgery limitations but still challenging enough to prepare me for the World Championship. My weekly training volume built gradually. My body was responding well. No back pain. No nerve symptoms. Just normal training soreness.

This time, I was doing everything right. No shortcuts. No pushing through warning signs. Just steady, consistent preparation for the race I had been chasing for over a decade. Training for Kona felt different from every other race. This wasn't just another IRONMAN race. This was *the* IRONMAN World Championship. The birthplace of the sport. The holy grail of endurance racing. The race that had seemed impossible when I could barely swim 37 yards.

My body was transforming again, becoming the efficient machine Kona would demand. The post-surgery weight came off gradually. My fitness built steadily. The weekly data showed consistent progress. But the real work wasn't just physical. I was preparing mentally and spiritually for what this race represented: the culmination of 12 years of training, setbacks, recoveries, and persistence.

Race Logistics

We booked flights to Hawaii for early October. I found a condo large enough for everyone—Andrea, the boys, and my parents. Everyone was coming to watch me race the World Championship.

I secured a bike travel case and nervously practiced disassembling and reassembling my bike. I ordered nutrition products in bulk, planning every gel and bottle I would need. I mapped out every detail of race week. The dream that had seemed so far away for so long was finally becoming real.

Hurricane Season

Then in August, hurricane season hit Florida with a vengeance. Hurricane Debby in early August knocked out power for a day and forced me to miss a key training ride. Hurricane Helene in late September swept through as I was supposed to be doing my final big training week: long ride, long run, final long swim. Instead, I was prepping for the storm.

Then Hurricane Milton, a direct hit on Tampa Bay that knocked out our power for five days, right when I should have been tapering and resting. My final big training week disappeared into storm recovery. Instead of logging miles, I was helping neighbors clean up debris, hauling tree limbs, and living without power.

I texted Scott, frustrated. "I'm missing critical training time. My taper is completely disrupted."

He responded, "You've already done the work. The hay is in the barn. Missing a few days of training two weeks before the race won't matter. What matters is that you stay healthy and don't get injured moving tree branches."

I wanted to believe him, but the lost training time was eating at me.

Still, I kept moving forward. The race was coming whether I felt perfectly prepared or not.

Kona Bound

On October 19, 2024, we loaded our bags and headed to the airport at 4:30 a.m. Our friend Ben picked us up to take us to the airport. Now every time I mention Ben to my family, the boys ask, "Are you talking about Airport Ben?" I guess he'll be forever known to us by that name.

Sitting in the airport waiting for our flight, I looked around at my family—Andrea, Jonathan, and Jaden—and thought of my parents also flying to Hawaii—all coming to support me in this crazy dream.

Twelve years since I could barely swim 37 yards.

Two back surgeries.

Fourteen IRONMAN race finishes.

Countless setbacks, recoveries, and moments of doubt.

And now, finally, we were Kona bound.

The journey had been longer than I had planned, harder than I had imagined, and more painful than I had expected.

But I didn't quit. I rebuilt. I learned. I adapted.

And now, the race I had visualized for over a decade was just days away.

Andrea asked, "How are you feeling?"

"Nervous. Excited. Thankful."

"You've earned this," she said. "Whatever happens out there, you've already won."

I knew what she meant. The real victory wasn't going to happen on race day. It had already happened in the daily discipline, in the refusal to quit after surgeries, in the slow rebuilding of my body and my purpose.

Kona was just the celebration of a journey that had already been won.

But I still wanted to finish.

And finish strong.

The plane lifted off, carrying us toward Hawaii, toward the race of a lifetime, toward the finish line I had been chasing since that salad bar meeting with Scott 12 years ago.

The impossible was about to become possible.

The Questions

What dream have you been chasing long enough to wonder if it will ever happen?

How do you maintain faith when setbacks keep pushing the finish line farther away?

Can you find meaning in the preparation even when the destination keeps shifting?

Sometimes the journey itself—the daily discipline, the refusal to quit, the rebuilding after each setback—becomes more significant than the destination you're chasing.

And sometimes, the person you become along the way matters more than the finish line you're racing toward.

2012 "before" photo—midnight video screenshot

2013 IRONMAN® Arizona 13 months of training and 50 pounds lighter

Coach Scott and me the day after IRONMAN® Arizona 2013

Jonathan, me, and Jaden IRONMAN® Arizona 2013

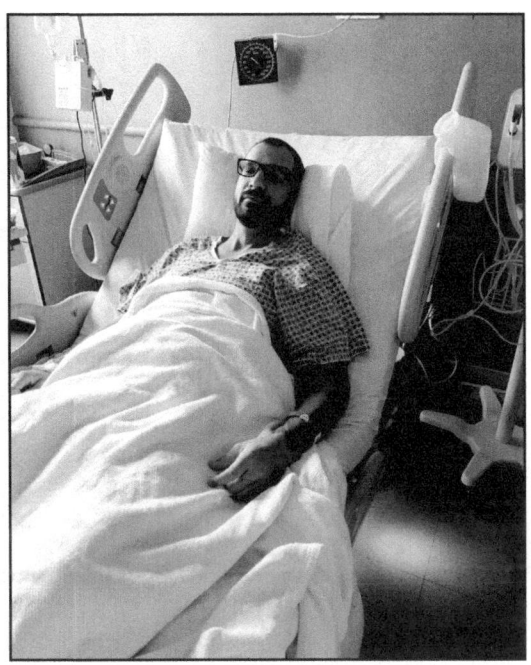

After first back surgery

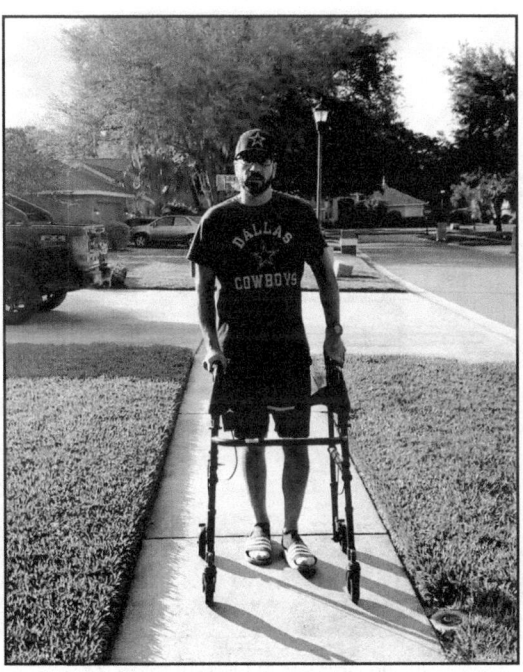

Post-surgery walk

Me and Andrea five months after first surgery IRONMAN® Waco, TX, 2022

Spring break 2023 Washington, DC

IRONMAN® World Championship Kona 2024

With my parents IRONMAN® World Championship Kona 2024

"Reunited" meeting with Coach Scott Rio Rancho, NM, 2025

Quandary Peak hike Colorado, 2025

IRONMAN® World Championship Nice, France, 2025

PART III

THE FINISH LINE

12

Race Week in Paradise

*"You are never too old to set another goal
or to dream a new dream."*
—C. S. LEWIS

The plane touched down in Kona around noon on Saturday, October 19, 2024. As we descended, I looked out at the volcanic landscape below, dark lava fields meeting the never-ending blue ocean, the kind of scenery that doesn't look real until you're standing in it.

Twelve years of chasing a dream that had nearly died on an operating table twice. And now we were here.

We picked up our rental van, large enough for all six of us, all our luggage, my bike case, and the mountain of nutrition products. The drive from the airport to our condo took us along the Queen Ka'ahumanu Highway, the legendary Queen K that I would be riding on race day.

"That's where I'll be biking," I said, pointing out the window.

"It looks hot," Jaden said.

He wasn't wrong. Even with the van's AC running, you could feel the heat radiating off the black lava fields. This was going to be a different kind of race than Louisville's humidity or Texas's wind. This was pure, unrelenting Hawaiian sun.

The boys were in the row behind us, already arguing about what to do first. My parents were flying in a little later that day. Everyone was excited to witness what they had supported from the beginning, back when I could barely swim 37 yards and the idea of an IRONMAN race seemed laughable.

"I can't believe we're actually here," Andrea said.

"I know," I said, still trying to believe it.

This wasn't just another race. This was Kona. The birthplace of IRONMAN. The place I had watched on television for years, wondering what it would feel like to stand on that starting line.

Now I was about to find out.

Our condo was perfect, spacious enough for everyone, large kitchen, close enough to transition that I wouldn't stress about logistics on race morning. We unpacked, and I immediately claimed a section of the living room for my gear staging area.

That first afternoon, we drove straight to the grocery store. This wasn't a vacation shopping trip; this was mission-critical nutrition. The boys still made a case that this was vacation shopping, throwing extra items in the cart. I had my list prepared, as every meal for the next week mattered. Every calorie needed to be accounted for.

At checkout, the cashier looked at our haul and smiled. "IRONMAN race?"

"How'd you know?" I asked.

"Your IRONMAN shirt and IRONMAN hat might have given it away."

She smiled and wished me good luck.

This whole town understood what we were here to do. Kona isn't just a race location; it's a community that embraces the insanity of people pushing themselves to extreme limits.

Back at the condo, I prepped some meals while Andrea started unpacking her bags. This was our rhythm after years of racing. She managed certain logistics while I managed race logistics, each of us carrying our part of the load. Only this time the boys were now old enough to take care of their own luggage.

That evening, we walked through Kona town. The place was transformed, IRONMAN banners everywhere, athletes in IRONMAN gear filling every restaurant and coffee shop. The buzz of nervous energy was all around us.

I felt simultaneously inspired and intimidated. These weren't weekend warriors. These were 2,100 of the world's fastest triathletes who had qualified by finishing in around nine hours, plus 300 Legacy Athletes like me who'd earned their spots through persistence rather than speed.

"You are going to do awesome," Andrea said, reading my mind again.

"I hope so! These people are legit athletes."

"You've done 14 IRONMAN races, had two back surgeries, and come back both times. You are more than ready!"

Practice Swim

Sunday morning, Andrea and I drove to Kailua Pier for the official practice swim. They had a full setup: wave starts, color-coded caps, and a cannon start. I wasn't just nervous. I was speechless. I was actually in Kona.

The cannon fired for the swim start, and I entered the water. The temperature was a perfect 78 degrees, warm without being bathwater hot like Louisville. The water was crystal clear and deep, like swimming in an aquarium. Bright tropical fish surrounded me, pulling my attention away from the fact that I was swimming 2.4 miles. At the turnaround buoy, the ocean floor dropped to around 150 feet, and I could almost see the bottom. A pod of dolphins swam beneath us. Six of them. Unreal.

I swam easily, not pushing, just enjoying the experience. At one point I stopped and started treading water to just look at everything around me. This practice swim wasn't about training; it was about soaking in the moment, about being present in this place I had dreamed of for so long.

As I approached the exit, volunteers stood waist-deep in the water, helping each swimmer out and placing a wooden practice-swim medal around our necks. Even the practice swim felt legendary.

"How was it?" Andrea asked when I found her on shore.

"There were dolphins. And the water was so clear. I still can't believe this is really happening."

We took a few pictures with my first medal for the week. This was her Kona as much as mine. Every race I had done, she'd been there cheering me on. This was the culmination of both our sacrifices.

Athlete Check-In

We then went to IRONMAN Village for athlete check-in. Vendors everywhere, athletes picking up race packets, photo opportunities with the iconic race signage.

I showed my ID at registration and received my race packet: bib number, timing chip, race information, and the coveted athlete wristband that would grant me access to transition all week.

"How do you feel?" the volunteer asked.

"Nervous," I admitted.

"Go have the race of your life."

Adventures

That afternoon, we loaded everyone into the van and drove the bike course. All 112 miles of it.

"We're driving the whole thing?" Jonathan asked.

"Every mile," I confirmed.

Our first stop was Kaloko-Honokōhau National Historical Park, where ancient Hawaiian fish ponds and petroglyphs told stories of people who'd lived on this island long before anyone thought to swim, bike, and run 140.6 miles in one day. Then Kīholo Bay, where impossibly turquoise water met black lava rock. Then Moʻokini Heiau, an ancient Hawaiian temple.

"Can you say that name?" Jaden asked.

We all tried. Our Southern accents butchered every Hawaiian word we attempted. The boys thought it was hilarious. Even in the midst of prerace intensity, there was room for laughter.

We reached Hawi, the bike turnaround point at mile 56, and stopped for lunch at Hawi & Kohala Coffee Mill. The food was incredible, but I was more focused on the realization that I would have to climb to this point on race day. Looking back at the road we had driven, I could see the elevation clearly now. Long, sustained climbs with occasional rollers. Nothing impossibly steep, but relentless. And I had trained in Florida, where the biggest hill is a highway overpass.

We continued our drive through the scenic countryside. Pololū Valley Lookout, with its stunning coastal views, the ranchlands around Waimea, and finally dinner at The Fish and The Hog, where I ate more than I probably should have but justified it as "carb-loading."

On the drive back to Kona as the sun set, Jonathan asked, "Dad, how are you feeling?"

"Scared half to death," I admitted.

"Ah, this is nothing. You've got this."

This was Kona. I wanted our boys to see that they could do anything they put their minds to if they refused to quit. Not only in racing, but in life. When things get hard, and they will get hard, I want them to remember that their dad never gave up.

Monday brought adventure as we drove to the lush east side of the island to explore waterfalls and valleys. Waipi'o Valley, where steep cliffs dropped to a black sand beach. 'Akaka Falls, with its 442-foot cascade. Rainbow Falls, where spray created perpetual rainbows. Boiling Pots and Kaumana Caves. Lunch at Pineapples Island Fresh Cuisine in Hilo was great.

That evening brought one of the most memorable experiences of the week: night snorkeling with manta rays. We gathered at the dock after sunset, put on snorkel gear, hopped on a boat, and then swam a short distance out to a floating platform illuminated by underwater lights. The lights attracted plankton, which attracted the manta rays. We held on to the PVC frame with pool noodles keeping our legs up, faces in the water, and waited.

Then they appeared.

Manta rays with wingspans of five to eight feet glided beneath us, so close I could have reached down and touched them. They performed graceful barrel rolls inches from our faces, their massive bodies moving with impossible elegance. One flipped directly under me, its white belly filling my entire field of vision, its wing tip brushing so close to my chest I felt the water displacement.

It was surreal. A reminder that this week wasn't just about suffering through 140.6 miles; it was about experiencing something pretty awesome that we would remember for the rest of our lives.

"That was so cool," Jaden said in the van afterward.

"Best thing we've done all week," Jonathan agreed.

And they were right. In the midst of all my race obsessing, this moment of pure wonder with my family mattered more than any training session.

Tuesday morning, I rode part of the Queen K on my bike. I needed to feel the road beneath my tires, experience the hills firsthand, understand what I would face on race day. The hills were not as intimidating as they had looked from the van. Not steep, but constant. False flats that looked easy but would still drain your legs. And the wind, the famous Kona trade winds that could either help or destroy your race depending on direction and timing. I rode for an hour, then turned back before pushing too hard. The goal was to feel the course, not to add training stress days before the race.

That afternoon, I attended the Legacy Athlete reception, 300 athletes who had completed at least 12 IRONMAN races, all gathering to celebrate the persistence that had brought us here. The outdoor pavilion area was filled with stories. Athletes in their 60s and 70s who had been racing for decades. People who had overcome cancer, heart attacks, and major accidents. Stories of setbacks and comebacks that made my two back surgeries seem almost routine.

Four IRONMAN champions spoke to all of us. These were legends of the sport who'd won Kona multiple times. Their advice was simple: Trust your training. Race your race. Don't let the moment overwhelm you. Remember why you started.

I sat there thinking about Scott and that salad bar meeting 12 years ago. About Andrea believing in me when I didn't believe in myself. About Coach Elizabeth teaching me how to fuel properly. About my parents supporting this crazy dream. About the boys growing up watching their dad chase something impossible.

This wasn't just my race. It was ours.

Wednesday morning brought my final run, an easy 30-minute shakeout to keep my legs active without depleting energy reserves. The heat was no joke, even in the early morning, worse than Florida, and I made a mental note to adjust my race-day expectations for the marathon.

That afternoon, we drove south to see the volcanoes. We visited Pu'uhonua o Hōnaunau National Historical Park, drove to the southernmost point in the United States, watched turtles sunbathe on black sand beaches, and explored Volcanoes National Park—active steam vents, the Kīlauea overlook, and lava tubes. The landscape was impressive, hardened lava fields stretching for miles, steam rising from cracks in the earth, the constant reminder that this island was alive and still forming.

Thursday evening brought the athlete briefing. The production was incredible. Full stage setup with massive LED walls showing course maps and elevation profiles. Concert-quality lighting and sound. This wasn't a typical race briefing; it was a show designed to pump up athletes and remind us we were part of something significant.

Out of nearly 100 countries represented, 2,100 of the world's fastest triathletes and 300 Legacy Athletes were all here to race and live out a dream. The energy was electric, nervous, excited, and focused.

Race officials went over everything: swim course details, bike cutoff times, transition procedures, what to expect on race day, safety protocols, how to handle the heat, hydration strategies, and the importance of listening to your body. I took notes as if I was studying for a final exam, though I had already memorized every detail from months of obsessive research.

I had done the work. The hay was in the barn, as Scott would often say.

Friday was for rest, though "rest" is relative when your mind is running through race scenarios on repeat.

We lounged at the condo. My parents took the boys to the beach. Andrea and I sat by the pool, and she asked the question I had been asking myself:

"How do you feel?"

"Ready. Scared. Overwhelmed. All of it."

"That sounds about right."

"What if something goes wrong? What if my back doesn't hold up?"

"Then you'll handle it. You always do."

"What if I don't finish?"

"You will finish. You've come too far not to."

She said it with such certainty that I almost believed it.

That afternoon, I went down to transition around 3 p.m. to rack my bike and drop off my gear bags. The transition area had hundreds of bikes being racked, athletes running through mental checklists, volunteers directing traffic, announcements echoing over loudspeakers.

I found my assigned spot, number marked clearly on the bike rack, and secured my bike. I hung my T1 and T2 bags on their designated hooks and triple-checked tire pressure one final time. Then I stood there for a moment, looking at it all. My bike, ready for 112 miles. My gear bags, packed perfectly. My timing chip, waiting to record every second of the journey.

The Moment

Twelve years had led to this moment. Every training session. Every setback. Every surgery. Every doubt. All of it had been necessary to bring me here.

"You good?" a volunteer asked.

"Yeah," I said. "I'm good."

I walked back to meet Andrea outside of transition. We held hands walking back to the van, not saying much. There wasn't much left to say. Everything had been done. All that remained was the race itself.

That night, I tried to sleep but mostly just stared at the ceiling, running through the race in my mind. The swim start. The first hill on the bike. The turnaround at Hawi. The long grind back to Kona. The marathon heat. The final miles on Ali'i Drive. The finish line.

Tomorrow at 6:45 a.m., the cannon would fire. And everything I had trained for, everything I had sacrificed, everything I had overcome, would all come down to one day—140.6 miles between me and becoming an IRONMAN World Championship finisher.

I prayed. Not for a fast time or even a good race. For the strength to finish. For my back to hold up. For my body to cooperate. For faith to carry me when strength ran out.

I was as ready as I would ever be.

The Questions

What preparation in your life feels as if it's leading to something significant?

How do you balance the intensity of chasing a dream with being present for the people who support you?

When you finally reach the starting line of something you've chased for years, how do you quiet the doubts and trust your preparation?

13

Kona—The Race of a Lifetime

"Success seems to be largely a matter of hanging on after others have let go."
—WILLIAM FEATHER

The alarm sounded at 3:30 a.m., pulling me from restless half-sleep into the darkness of race morning. October 26, 2024. The day I had been chasing for 12 years. I lay there for a moment, listening to Andrea moving around the room getting ready. I was trying to process that this was actually happening. After everything, the addiction to energy drinks, the two back surgeries, the countless setbacks, the delayed dreams, I was about to race the IRONMAN World Championship in Kona, Hawaii.

I got up and went to the kitchen to prepare my prerace breakfast. Two packets of oatmeal with maple syrup, a banana, and a bottle of Skratch sports drink. My stomach was tight with nerves, but I forced the food down. My body would need every calorie over the next 14 to 17 hours.

Andrea appeared in the doorway, already dressed. She was ready to begin her own IRONMAN race day, tracking me, navigating crowds, keeping the family organized, cheering at strategic points.

"Ready?" she asked.

"As I'll ever be."

The boys emerged next, sleepy but excited. My parents came out a few minutes later. Team Millsaps was all in, everyone awake before 4 a.m. to support this crazy dream. All of them were proudly wearing their matching overpriced IRONMAN merchandise. We loaded into the van and drove toward downtown Kona. The streets were already filled with athletes and spectators, all moving to the starting area. Car headlights cut through the humid air, and I could feel my heart rate climbing.

"You've got this," my oldest said from the back seat.

"Thanks, buddy."

"Seriously, Dad. You've trained for this. Just don't stop."

Simple wisdom when I needed it most.

We found parking close to transition, and I gathered my special-needs bags and final nutrition items. The energy around me was electric, thousands of people moving with nervous purpose, athletes doing last-minute equipment checks, volunteers shouting directions, the hum of organized chaos.

I walked through the crowd toward my bike, checking my watch even though I knew exactly what time it was. My transition spot looked exactly as I had left it yesterday, bike secure, bags hanging, everything ready.

I dropped my special-needs bags into the designated boxes that would later be placed out on the course, then made my way toward Kailua Pier for the swim start.

The sky was beginning to lighten, painting everything in soft predawn colors. The ocean looked calm, almost peaceful, which felt at odds with the nervous energy coursing through my body.

After the national anthem and a special Hawaiian drum presentation, which I barely heard over my pounding heartbeat, and final race instructions from the announcer, they began calling age groups to enter the water.

The pros went first at 6:25 a.m. Then age groupers began entering in waves, organized by our ages. I was in the 40–44 age group. My group wouldn't start until 7:10 a.m., which meant 45 minutes of waiting, watching, and trying not to let anxiety spiral.

The water was warm as I waded in, 78 degrees, perfect temperature. I treaded water with my age group, waiting for the horn, surrounded by hundreds of other athletes doing the same nervous dance of anticipation. Kayak volunteers patrolled the starting area, making sure no one jumped the gun. We floated there, bobbing in the gentle swell, staring at the starting line marked by buoys and a line of kayaks paddling back and forth. Then I felt it, a sharp sting on my tricep. Jellyfish. I looked around and saw them everywhere—small, translucent creatures drifting in the current like unwelcome party guests. Several guys near me were getting stung, asking each other if they had been hit too.

"Yeah, I got nailed," the guy next to me said, rubbing his face where a tentacle had apparently brushed him.

But there was no time to worry about jellyfish. The horn was about to sound.

I took a deep breath and focused on what was ahead: 2.4 miles of swimming through some of the most beautiful water on earth.

The Race

The horn blasted. "Let's go-o-o!" I yelled, along with a hundred other voices, and put my face in the water. Arms and legs everywhere, but with enough space that I didn't get the aquatic beating I had experienced in other races. I settled into my stroke quickly, focusing on long pulls and steady breathing.

The water clarity was stunning. I could see everything—coral formations below, schools of bright tropical fish darting past, the ocean floor dropping away to darker depths. At one point, I looked down and saw them again: dolphins.

A pod of dolphins appeared again—six graceful creatures gliding beneath us like they were escorting the race. One swam directly under me, maybe 20 feet down, its body moving with such effortless power that I felt inadequate trying to swim above it.

I kept my sighting disciplined, every six strokes, quick head lift to check the buoys, then back to swimming. The jellyfish sting on my arm burned with each stroke, but I tried to ignore it. Another discomfort in a day that would be full of discomforts.

I passed the second turn and began the final stretch back toward shore. My arms were tired but not exhausted. My breathing was steady. The swim was going well.

A little over an hour and 20 minutes after entering the water, I reached the stairs at the swim exit. Two volunteers grabbed my hands and helped me out, and I jogged toward transition.

A volunteer with a spray bottle called out, "Jellyfish stings? Jellyfish stings?"

I raised my arm. "Right here."

He sprayed my tricep, and the smell hit immediately: vinegar. I even got some of the spray that missed my arm directly in my mouth! Definitely vinegar. The sting would still burn for hours.

T1 was a blur of practiced motions. I grabbed my bike gear bag from the rack, found a folding chair in the massive changing tent filled with men in various states of undress (I kept my eyes firmly on my own gear), and transformed from swimmer to cyclist.

I dried off my feet. Socks on. Bike shoes Velcroed. Helmet secured. PBJ sandwiches shoved in my back pockets. Everything felt good. My back felt stable.

I grabbed my bike from the rack and jogged toward the mount line, where thousands of spectators lined the barriers, cheering for each athlete passing by, professional production cameras set up on elevated platforms. The energy was intoxicating. I swung my leg over my bike, clipped in, hit the lap button on my Garmin, and started the 112-mile journey. Here we go. This is Kona. This is everything.

My nutrition plan was precise and memorized:

- Hour 0–1: Half bottle Infinit (double concentration), half bottle Nuun electrolytes, water at aid stations
- Hour 1–2: PB&J sandwich, half bottle Nuun, water
- Hour 2–3: Half bottle Infinit, half bottle Nuun, water

- Hour 3–4: Clif Bar, half bottle Nuun, water
- Special-needs bag at mile 56
- Repeat pattern for second half

I stuck to the plan like my life depended on it, because in a way, it did. Nutrition mistakes in an IRONMAN race don't show up immediately; they show up hours later when your body shuts down and you're still 60 miles from the finish.

The first 30 miles felt strong. The Queen K stretched before me, the legendary highway I had watched on television for years. Rolling terrain where nothing looked steep but everything cost you, and the relentless sun turning the black lava fields into a furnace.

The jellyfish sting on my arm continued burning with every movement, but I compartmentalized it. Pain was information. It wasn't stopping me.

I saw Andrea and the boys at a spectator spot. They were screaming and ringing cowbells, and that brief moment of connection gave me a surge of energy. I wasn't alone out here.

Then, around mile 40, everything changed.

The wind hit.

The legendary Kona trade winds arrived with fury, and suddenly I was pedaling hard to maintain 8 mph. Then 6 mph. The wind roared against me, grinding my forward progress to a crawl. I looked around at other cyclists, all of us with the same confused expression: Are we even moving?

This was the Kona that breaks people. Not the heat alone, not the hills alone, but the wind that makes every mile feel like three.

I dropped into my easiest gear and kept turning the pedals. No point fighting what I couldn't control. I needed to survive this section and hope the wind would shift. The climb toward Hawi seemed endless. Mile after mile of grinding uphill into a headwind, watching my speed hover between 6 and 8 mph, burning through energy reserves faster than I had planned.

Several times out on the bike, I remembered why I was there. Twelve years of training. Two back surgeries. My family watching. The people who had followed my journey. Scott believing in me when I couldn't swim 37 yards. And my pastor back home following me on the tracker; a man who would absolutely never let me live it down if I quit.

So I kept pedaling.

Finally, I reached the turnaround at Hawi. The little town was packed with spectators, all cheering despite the heat. I slowed way down, made the turn, and faced what I had been waiting for: mostly downhill with a tailwind. The relief was immediate. My speed jumped to 20 mph, then 25. I tucked into the aero position and let the road carry me back toward Kona.

The climb and headwind had cost me time and energy I would need later. My nutrition had fallen slightly behind schedule because I had been so focused on surviving the wind.

I made it back into Kona, where I was welcomed by thousands of people. Everyone was cheering, which felt like it was for me. Cowbells ringing, air horns, custom poster boards. My speed naturally picked up, and the pain I had felt for the last 6½ hours immediately left my body. I was feeling strong.

I dismounted from my bike and rolled it into the transition. I grabbed my run gear bag and sat down for a few minutes to catch my breath and gather my thoughts. I downed an orange Gatorade, ate a bag of Lay's potato chips, and took in one more gel. I was already sick of these little gels. I put on clean socks, laced up my running shoes, put on my race bib, grabbed my bottle of Skratch, and shoved about 10 gels in my pocket for the run.

I left transition and ran through a sea of people. I was looking around for my family, but I couldn't find them. We ran down the road and then made a turnaround to start running out toward the energy lab. While still in town after the first turn, I heard my family cheering on the side of the road. I made my way over to them and stopped to say hi. I had seven hours to finish this race, so I had plenty of time.

My two sons immediately said, "Why are you stopping?" I told them, "Because I'm hot and tired." Andrea gave me a quick kiss, and my parents wished me luck as they were trying to take more pictures of me with their phones. Andrea yelled one more time, *"You're doing great! Keep it up!"*

My run nutrition plan was:

1 bottle of Skratch per hour

1 gel every 15 to 20 minutes, depending on pace

In my special-needs bag, I had more Skratch to fill my bottle, a PB&J, a Clif Bar, Vaseline, and chafing cream.

I did my best to stick with my nutrition plan for the run, but I was ready for some real food, like pizza and ice cream.

The run was hot. I stopped at every aid station, ice down my suit, cold sponges, fluids. I ran next to a guy from Austria for a few miles, and as we talked, it helped make the miles go by quicker.

I had to stop at a porta-potty, and by this time, these things had been well used and were pretty gross. I stepped inside and laughed, remembering a race in Knoxville when an older lady had exited the porta-potty and told me she couldn't figure out the little sink inside. I realized later, she had tried to wash her hands in the urinal. That memory still cracks me up.

The sun was setting, and the heat was finally letting up. It even rained a little on the run, which was nice and refreshing. We entered the dark stretch near the energy lab. Few lights. I followed shoe reflectors. Mile 20, I walked. Mile 23, I was energized like at the start of the race.

I took off. I was going to run the rest of this race and run it hard. I was close to breaking a 14-hour IRONMAN race and knew if I could keep this pace, I would accomplish that time.

I could see the huge tree on the final turn before you hit the finish chute. My feet hit the red carpet where flags from every country lined the path ahead. The crowd was cheering, and I could see the finish line. This was it. This was what I had been training for and looking toward for over a decade. I had a lump in my throat knowing all that

I had been through to get to this point. All the years, all the pain, all the doubt; it was behind me now.

As I approached the finish line, the announcer said those famous words: "From Tampa, Florida, Jason Millsaps, you are an IRONMAN!"

I crossed the line and stopped under the LED banner, arms still raised, trying to process what had just happened.

Official time: 13:58:34.

I did it. After two back surgeries. After countless setbacks. After delays and disappointments. After 12 years of chasing this dream.

I was an IRONMAN World Championship finisher.

Postrace

A volunteer caught me, asked if I was okay, draped a medal around my neck, and wrapped me in an IRONMAN Kona towel. I nodded and said yes.

The medal was heavy. Substantial, but more than a medal and ribbon, it represented everything I had overcome to get here.

I walked through the finisher area in a daze, accepting congratulations from other athletes, all of us sharing the same exhausted joy.

Then I found them: Andrea and the boys, my parents, all of them smiling, cheering, and proud.

We hugged, and Andrea said loudly, "You did it. I knew you would."

"We did it," I corrected. "This is ours."

Because it was. Every doubt I had, she believed in me anyway. Every setback, she helped me rebuild.

This medal belonged to both of us.

Both boys were beaming, and deep down they were proud. You could see it on their faces.

"Way to go, Dad."

"Thanks, buddy."

Standing there with my family, medal around my neck, body completely spent, I tried to comprehend that the dream I had been chasing since that salad bar meeting with Scott had finally come true.

That night, back at the condo with everyone finally asleep, every muscle in my body ached, but it was the good kind of ache, the kind that comes from using everything you have to accomplish something meaningful.

The Reflection

I couldn't stop thinking about the journey: the wake-up call of seeing myself in that video. The 37 yards. Meeting Scott. The first triathlon. The first IRONMAN race. The surgeries. The long road back. The disappointment when Kona got delayed. The second surgery. The waiting. The training. And finally, today.

Twelve years of my life had been pointed toward this one day. And it had delivered everything I had ever hoped for and more.

The Truth

But more than the race itself, I was grateful for who I had become in the process. The discipline I had developed. The grit I had built. The example I had set for my sons. The relationship I had strengthened with Andrea through shared sacrifice.

This was true transformation.

So many times along this journey, I'd been reminded that faith in God carries you when strength runs out. That setbacks don't have to be endings. That ordinary people can accomplish extraordinary things when they refuse to quit. And this lesson, this truth, was worth every painful mile.

The Questions

What impossible thing have you been telling yourself you can't do?

What would change if you stopped focusing on why you're not qualified and started focusing on showing up anyway?

The finish line isn't the reward—it's proof that you never quit. The real victory is who you become in the struggle.

Your Kona is waiting. The only question is: Will you show up for the training required to reach it?

The Space Between

*"The bend in the road is not the end of the
road unless you refuse to take the turn."*
—AUTHOR UNKNOWN

The morning after Kona, I woke up sore in places I didn't know could be sore. My legs barely functioned. My back, surprisingly, felt okay; the hardware was holding. But everything else was pretty sore, to say the least. But this was normal the day after an IRONMAN race.

Andrea and the boys were already up, ready to take a puddle-jumper plane to another island now that the race was behind us. We spent the next few days being tourists, snorkeling, visiting beaches, riding WaveRunners, eating at local restaurants without obsessing over macros and calories. For those few days, I felt exactly how I had expected to feel: satisfied. Complete. I had done it. The dream that had consumed 12 years of my life was finished.

But then we flew home.

After I returned to Florida and we settled back into the reality of work and school, the medal hung on the wall in my office. I had achieved the goal that had driven me for 12 years. But underneath that satisfaction, something else stirred. A question I hadn't prepared for:

Now what?

For 12 years, my life had been calibrated by forward motion. Training six days a week. Races on the calendar. Goals on the wall.

IRONMAN racing wasn't just a sport or hobby; it was woven into the fabric of our family's rhythm.

My boys were almost 7 and 4 years old when I started my IRONMAN racing journey. Now they were 19 and 16, both driving, both nearly grown. They had spent their entire childhoods watching their dad wake up before dawn to swim, bike, and run. They knew what "taper week" meant. They had been on race-cations almost every year. They could track me on race apps better than I could.

When I crossed that finish line in Kona, I expected to feel complete. I had reached the summit. I was certain satisfaction would follow. After all, it was what I had trained for, talked about, posted about, prayed about. But instead of fulfillment, something else settled in: silence.

Not pride. Not relief. A strange quiet.

And then the question I hadn't trained for: *Now what?*

The Emptiness

People asked me what I was going to do next, and I would casually say, "I'm not sure yet, but I'll do something."

I really hadn't anticipated this feeling. I would put training sessions on my workout calendar. I would go for a long bike ride or a long swim. But I felt nothing. The spark was gone.

I wasn't physically tired. I was disoriented. It was the weirdest feeling. Almost depressing. It felt strange, because for years, my life had been defined by forward motion. I was the guy training for the next race, the next mountain, the next breakthrough. I was the guy who pushed through windstorms in Texas and heat exhaustion in Louisville.

I was always on the way to something.

Now I wasn't.

Andrea noticed before I said anything.

"You okay?" she asked one evening. "Yeah, just tired."

"Jason, you've been 'just tired' for four weeks. What's really going on?"

I didn't know how to explain it. "I thought finishing Kona would feel different. Like everything would make sense. Like I would feel . . . complete."

"And you don't?"

"I don't know what I feel. It's like I spent 12 years climbing a mountain, and now that I'm at the top, I don't know what to do up here."

She was quiet for a moment. "Maybe you're not supposed to stay at the top. Maybe the point was the climb."

"Then what do I do now? Climb down?"

"Or find a different mountain."

I wasn't even sure if I was correctly describing my feelings. Was I the only one who had experienced a feeling like this after achieving a big goal?

Maybe you've experienced this same feeling. Maybe you're a CEO who stepped down after 30 years of building a company, and now you don't know who you are without the title. Maybe you climbed the corporate ladder for years, reached VP or partner, and then realized you miss the passion you had starting out. Maybe you're a parent who spent decades raising kids, and the last one just left for college. The house is quiet. Your purpose feels gone. Maybe you spent years in a relationship that defined you, and now you're single again, wondering who you are without that person.

The Space

There comes a moment in every high achiever's life when the calendar goes quiet. No more races. No more meetings. No more countdowns to launch days, big goals, or finish lines.

Just space. Silence. And a strange ache where certainty used to live.

At first, I tried to fix it like a flat tire or a broken chain. That's my natural instinct. I did what I knew to do: I put workouts on the calendar even though I had no race to train for. I scrolled through race websites looking for the next goal, the next challenge, the next thing to chase.

But nothing felt right. Nothing sparked the same fire.

Andrea watched me mope around for a few weeks. I had never experienced this feeling before. "You don't have to figure this out today," she said. "Maybe you need to just sit in this for a while."

"Sit in what? Emptiness?"

"No. Sit in the quiet. Stop running from it."

Did she know who she was asking to sit still? Even my elementary school teachers would ask me to sit still all the time. But I didn't know how to sit still. I had trained my body to tolerate pain, to endure 140.6 miles on pure willpower. I was now learning that no one trains you for stillness. No one teaches you how to sit in the quiet and not immediately run toward the next medal.

One evening at dinner, Jonathan asked, "Dad, are you going to do another IRONMAN race?"

"I don't know. Maybe," I said. "I think I'm just figuring out what comes next."

Jaden jumped in. "What if nothing comes next? What if you're just . . . done?"

"Yeah, and you gain all your weight back!" Jonathan chimed in.

They are such an encouragement.

But deep down, those were all the questions and thoughts flooding my head.

What if I was done? What if 12 years of chasing IRONMAN finishes had run its course? What if the next chapter didn't involve racing at all? What if I just went back to my old habits?

The thought terrified me. Because if I wasn't a triathlete, who was I?

In October 2023, during my recovery from the second surgery, I had launched 121 Tri Coaching. I had the certifications. The website. The name. The vision.

But now, months later, I still didn't have any clients. I wasn't really pushing it, and I'm terrible at social media.

I started questioning everything. Was I a good enough coach? Did I have the credibility? Why would anyone pay me when there were coaches with decades more experience?

Andrea found me one night scrolling through other coaches' websites, comparing their credentials to mine.

"What are you doing?" she asked.

"Trying to figure out why my business isn't growing."

"Maybe because you're comparing yourself to people who've been coaching for 20 years, and you just started."

"But I now have 15 IRONMAN race finishes. I came back from two surgeries. Doesn't that count for something?"

"Of course it does. But you're sitting here comparing yourself with people who've been doing this for decades. You're not even sure what you want this to be yet."

Maybe she was right. Again.

The Lesson

If you're in that moment now, or will be soon, know that you are not broken. You are not lost. And most importantly, if you are still breathing, you are not done. You are in the space between stories. The space no one trains us for. There's a sacred tension in that space. It's uncomfortable. It feels like failure when it's actually transformation.

Once we get to this pivotal moment, we now have the option to choose a new purpose that isn't tied to performance, find a new rhythm that isn't defined by urgency, or build a new identity not rooted in doing, but in being. The finish line isn't the end. It's a turning point. A bend in the road. A graduation into a deeper kind of life.

I needed perspective beyond my own experience. Even if you aren't familiar with the Bible, in it there are many examples of leaders that God formed during the "space between." One night, unable to sleep, with my mind racing, I found myself thinking about stories in the Bible of people who waited. Who wandered. Who wondered if God had forgotten them.

Moses came to mind first. Moses spent 40 years tending sheep in the desert after running from his past of being a murderer in exile, far from the palace where he had grown up. Forty years. That's a long time to prepare for one moment. I had struggled through 12 years to get to Kona, and that felt like forever. Moses waited more than three times that long before God showed up at a burning bush. Those 40 years of tending sheep weren't wasted time; they were preparation for leading a nation through the wilderness. The realization hit me hard. What if my emptiness wasn't failure, but preparation?

There was another man, Joseph (not Mary's husband), who spent years in slavery and prison, waiting for God's plan to unfold (Genesis 39–41). He was betrayed by his brothers, falsely accused, forgotten in jail. The space between his dream and its fulfillment was brutal. But that space made him into the leader Egypt needed. Joseph's brothers meant his slavery for evil, but God meant it for good. I thought about my back surgeries. I had seen them as interruptions to my racing. What if they were actually preparation for coaching others through injury?

These weren't just ancient stories. They were mirrors showing me something I needed to see: Emptiness doesn't mean failure. Sometimes it means you're being prepared for something you can't yet imagine. Understanding this didn't immediately fix my post-Kona confusion. But it helped me stop fighting the quiet and start listening to what it might be teaching me. What if God does His deepest work not on the race course, but in the quiet after?

Helen Steiner Rice captured this truth in her poem "The Bend in the Road," reminding us that what looks like an ending is often just a turn we can't yet see. God's perspective reveals that our supposed dead ends are simply bends in the road leading somewhere new. Her words became a reminder that unseen paths often lead to deeper growth. I had been viewing Kona as the end. The summit. The destination. But what if it was just a bend? What if the real story was just beginning?

The same voice that carried me through mile 20 in Arizona was now calling me into something different: rest. *He makes me lie down*, Psalm 23:2 says. I had read those words a thousand times, had even sung them in worship services, but I had never really heard them.

I'm sure He whispered this during both of my surgeries; I just didn't listen then. I'm hard of hearing sometimes. My wife would call it selective listening. God sometimes has to make us lie down through injury, through exhaustion, through circumstances that force us to stop running. Both surgeries had been forced rest. This post-Kona emptiness felt like another. But this time, instead of fighting it, I wondered: What if I actually listened?

Around this time, I reread James Clear's *Atomic Habits*, and one line jumped out: "You do not rise to the level of your goals. You fall to the level of your systems." Goals are helpful, but they are short-term. They exist for people who want to win once. Systems—habits, routines, processes—are what keep you moving forward long after the goal is achieved.

The Shift

When I shifted from chasing goals to cultivating growth, everything changed. The finish line in Kona didn't have to be the end. It could be a marker on a much longer road. Growth doesn't expire. Growth keeps going. It isn't tied to one race, one medal, or one moment. It becomes a way of living, a rhythm that continues long after the applause fades.

Gradually, I began to see the "space between" not as emptiness, but as fertile ground. I tried to listen more, reflect on a deeper level, and ask different questions. What legacy am I building—not as a triathlete, but as a husband, father, mentor, and friend? What would it look like to define success not by finish times, but by who I'm becoming? What if the best parts of my life are still ahead, in ways I can't yet imagine?

Maybe this was the finish line that mattered most. Not in Kona, but here. Not in pain, but in peace. Not in medals, but in meaning. I was almost ready to let go. I felt like I was slowly learning how to live without a race on the calendar, without a goal driving every decision, without the constant need to prove something.

And then came the unexpected.

On March 5, 2025, an email landed in my inbox:

Bonjour,

As a 2024 IRONMAN Legacy Program athlete who has already raced at the IRONMAN World Championship in Kona and contributed to the rich history of IRONMAN, we are thrilled to offer you a special opportunity to race at the 2025 IRONMAN World Championship in Nice, France.

We can't wait to see you in Nice.

I read it three times.

Then I texted Andrea a screenshot.

My heart surged, not with the desperate need I had felt before Kona, but with something different. Lighter. Joy.

"What do you think?" I texted.

Her response came immediately: "I think you already know."

She was right. I did know.

But this time, it was different.

I wasn't racing to prove something. I wasn't racing because my identity depended on it. I wasn't racing to fill the void or answer the question "Now what?"

I was racing because I wanted to. Because it sounded fun. Because France with my bride sounded like an adventure.

One week later, I registered.

IRONMAN race number 16. One more World Championship. This time in Nice, France.

But this race wouldn't be about validation or culmination or proving I could come back from surgeries.

This race would be about joy.

The Truth

If your worth depends on what you accomplish, you'll never feel secure. Because every achievement eventually fades. Every medal tarnishes. Every finish line becomes a starting line for the next race. You'll spend your whole life running from the fear that you're not enough.

It's important to remember that stillness is not the enemy. For years, I equated motion with progress. I had lived with the lie that I always had to be working. If I wasn't training, I wasn't growing. But some of the most important growth happens when you stop moving long enough to listen.

The purpose that drives you at 35 might not be the purpose that sustains you at 47. That's not failure. That's growth. The question isn't "What was I made to do?" The question is "What am I being called to do now?"

Every finish line I crossed prepared me to coach someone else to theirs. Every setback I overcame taught me how to help someone else overcome theirs. Nothing is wasted if you're willing to pass it forward. Sometimes the best way to honor what you've achieved is to help others achieve it too.

So yes, I registered for Nice. But not because I needed another medal. Not because I was trying to fill the void Kona left. I registered because the space between had taught me how to race differently.

And somewhere in that space between Kona and Nice, something unexpected happened: I actually started coaching athletes. During the summer while training for Nice, I signed on my first athlete. Real people. Real goals. Real trust that I could help them reach finish lines that once seemed impossible to them.

The Athletes

One athlete, a woman, is training for IRONMAN 70.3 Florida in Haines City, my very first half. Every time I write her training plan, I think about standing on that beach with alligator warning signs, terrified and underprepared but refusing to quit.

Another athlete, I'll call him Pete, is preparing for his first full IRONMAN race. The location? Tempe, Arizona. The same place where my IRONMAN race journey began in 2013. Pete's been training hard, maybe too hard, pushing through every workout like the race depends on perfection rather than preparation.

I recently found myself having a conversation with him that felt oddly familiar.

"The hay is in the barn," I told him over the phone. "Missing a few workouts this close to race day won't hurt you. What will hurt is showing up injured or overtrained." The words came out of my mouth, and I heard Scott. The same words he had spoken to me before Arizona. Before Texas. Before every race when my anxiety tried to convince me I hadn't done enough. Now I was the one saying them. Passing forward what had been given to me.

And then there's the athlete I spoke with who might be my favorite story yet. He had lost significant weight, completely transformed his life, and finished 16 IRONMAN races over the years. Sixteen. This past year, he finally received the email he had been chasing: an invitation to race Kona as a Legacy Athlete.

When he told me, I felt the same surge of emotion I had felt opening my own Kona invitation. Because I knew what that moment meant. Not just the race itself, but everything it represented: the years of showing up, the refusal to quit, the quiet accumulation of miles that nobody sees but everybody feels at the finish line.

Full Circle

The guy who could barely swim 37 yards was now coaching others toward their own impossible dreams. The medals on my wall weren't the end of the story; they were preparation for this: helping someone else believe they could do what they once thought they couldn't. Maybe that's what the space between was really about. Not emptiness, but apprenticeship. Not loss of purpose, but discovery of a bigger one.

This time, I would race from strength, not weakness.

From joy, not desperation. From gratitude, not need.

The Mediterranean. The mountain roads. The French Riviera. The bike course used in the Tour de France.

I wasn't chasing validation. I was responding to a gift.

One more chance not to prove something, but to live something.

The space between had taught me to breathe differently—slower, deeper, with more trust.

And so it was back to training. But this time, training felt different. Lighter. More like play than work.

Because I finally understood:

The race isn't the destination. The race is part of the journey.

And the journey doesn't end at a finish line.

It just continues, one mile at a time, toward something bigger than any medal could ever represent.

The Questions

What do you do when you achieve the goal you've been chasing for years?

How do you find purpose after reaching the summit you thought was the destination?

Is the emptiness that sometimes follows achievement a sign that you chose the wrong goal, or an invitation to choose a bigger game?

Maybe real growth doesn't happen when you're chasing the dream; it happens when you decide what to do after catching it.

And maybe the best part of your story isn't the achievement itself; it's what you build in the space that comes after.

15

Nice—Racing from Joy

"Perseverance is not a long race;
it is many short races one after the other."
—WALTER ELLIOT

When I registered for Nice, France, something was different from every other race I had ever signed up for. No anxiety. No desperate need to prove something. No fear that my identity depended on the outcome. Just a simple thought: *This sounds fun.*

After 12 years of racing toward something—validation, transformation, redemption, Kona—I was finally racing *from* something: joy. Strength. Gratitude. Kona was the mountain I climbed to prove I could. Nice would be the mountain I climbed because I wanted to. And that shift changed everything.

I mapped out a detailed training plan for Nice, but this time, I built it differently. Instead of asking life to pause for training, I wove training into life.

Our church leadership blessed our family with an eight-week sabbatical after 10 years of ministry. This rare gift gave me space to rest, recharge, travel with Andrea and the boys, sit with mentors, worship in churches across the country, and read books that both challenged and encouraged me. It also gave me a looser schedule for workouts.

Training for Nice didn't feel like the grind it had been for Kona. It felt freer. Something I looked forward to instead of something I had to check off.

Quandary Peak

Travel during my sabbatical meant I was sometimes without a bike. So I improvised. While visiting Colorado, I convinced Andrea and Jaden to tackle a 14er with me: Quandary Peak, 14,271 feet.

We set out at 6 a.m., determined to summit before afternoon thunderstorms rolled in. The air was crisp, the trail steep, and the views already stunning at the lower elevations. By 12,000 feet, everything changed. The air thinned. Breathing became harder. Our pace slowed to less than 1 mph.

At 12,500 feet, Andrea stopped. "How far have we gone?"

"A mile and a half."

She looked at Jaden, who was also struggling. "I think this is our limit. You should keep going. We'll head back down and meet you at the trailhead."

I hesitated. "You sure?"

"Yes. Go finish. We'll be fine."

So I kept climbing.

The final stretch was brutal. Unstable boulders, calf-deep snow in sections, and nearly everyone I passed wearing crampons (spikes for traction). I was in running shoes. Not my smartest move. But I could see the summit. And I wasn't turning back. Step by step, breath by breath, I kept moving forward.

When I finally reached the top, I stood there taking in a 360-degree panoramic view of ridgelines stretching in every direction. You can't describe what it feels like to stand on top of a mountain like that. You just have to experience it.

I snapped photos, shot a video, and then started the long descent back to Andrea and Jaden. When I reached the trailhead, Andrea announced her retirement from 14ers, and Jaden wanted to know what was for lunch.

That mountain taught me something important: Watch your footing. Breathe even when the air is thin. And keep moving toward the view only the summit can give.

Nice was going to require the same mindset.

Nutrition Check-In

With 14 weeks to race day, I checked in with Coach Elizabeth about nutrition. Post-Kona, my body composition had shifted slightly, and I wanted to ensure that I was fueling optimally for the demands of the Nice course.

Elizabeth reviewed my training log alongside my nutrition patterns and identified something counterintuitive: I wasn't eating enough to support my training load. This is a common mistake among endurance athletes. We think optimization requires eating less, when actually it requires eating strategically to support the work. She helped me understand that on high-volume training days, my body needed significantly more carbohydrates to fuel performance and recovery. Under-fueling wasn't helping; it was increasing injury risk and compromising adaptation.

We adjusted my approach: moderate intake on easier days, substantial fueling before and during long sessions, and prioritizing protein for recovery. The focus shifted from restriction to optimization. From controlling to fueling.

The Fall

Twenty-one days out from race day, the nerves returned. You would think after 15 IRONMAN races, the anxiety would fade. But this race felt different. Not worse, just different. The mountains of Nice loomed in my mind. The grinding climbs. The hair-raising descents. More than for medals or times, my prayer was simple: *Make the cutoffs. Finish healthy. Cross the finish line strong.*

My taper had begun, and that morning's plan was an easy 10-mile run before work. At 4:50 a.m., I stepped out the door and started down the dark sidewalk. Not even a mile in, my toe caught the uneven lip of the concrete. In an instant, I flew across the pavement—more of a slide than a fall. My water bottle went flying as I crashed hard on my elbow and palms. A car passed by, and I wondered if the driver even noticed the guy sprawled across the pavement. I scrambled to my feet, dusted off, found the bottle, and stood there debating: limp home or push through?

I chose to keep going.

Unfortunately, this wasn't the first time I had fallen during training. When I returned home, I showed Andrea the scrapes on my arm.

She shook her head. "You fell again?"

"Yup."

"You know, I might need to hold your hand on all our walks when we're old."

"Maybe start now," I said.

She just smiled and deep down knew that was probably the truth.

The Nerves

The nerves still lingered. So I pulled up my training data from last year's Kona build and compared it to this year. To my relief, the numbers didn't lie: I was fitter, stronger, and better prepared for Nice than I had been for Kona. That was good news. But it didn't silence the anxiety entirely.

Maybe part of that nervousness wasn't about the race at all. Maybe it was knowing the "space between" was coming again, that strange silence that follows the finish line. The questions would return: *What's next?*

I had to remind myself of the shift I had made. James Clear wrote: *"Goals are for people who want to win once. Systems are for people who want to keep winning."*

This race wasn't about checking off number 16. It was about continuing to grow, to live differently.

As with most things, it's easy to slip back into old ways, chasing medals instead of transformation.

I had to choose growth again.

Nice, France

Packing my bags once again, I found myself preparing for another adventure—my first international race and my second IRONMAN World Championship—11 months after Kona. And once again, Airport Ben picked us up to take us to the airport.

We touched down early Tuesday morning, exhausted but excited. That excitement quickly turned to panic when we reached baggage claim and my bike was nowhere to be found. After a frantic search, we learned that it had taken an unplanned detour to Germany. The airline promised it would arrive the next morning and be delivered to our hotel. It wasn't the kind of start I had hoped for. With my nerves already stretched tight, this setback only made things worse.

Andrea and I tried to make the most of the day, wandering through the cobblestone streets of Old Town Nice, soaking in its charm, and walking along the pebble-covered Mediterranean shore. The sea reflected the sun in the afternoon light, and for a moment, I let myself relax.

"This is beautiful," Andrea said, looking out at the water.

"Yeah. Very different from Kona."

"Everything about this feels different," she observed.

She was right. Kona had been intense, focused, heavy with the weight of a 12-year dream. Nice felt . . . different. Like we were actually on vacation, sort of, and the race just happened to be part of it.

"Are you nervous?" she asked.

"Terrified. But also really excited. Does that make sense?"

"Perfect sense."

Wednesday morning brought the practice swim, a structured 1.2-mile race across the bay. The water temperature was 77 degrees, too warm for wetsuits, so I zipped into my swim skin and lined up with hundreds of other athletes. The air horn blasted, and suddenly I was slicing through water so clear and salty it reminded me of blue

Gatorade. It was stunning. My stroke felt smooth. When I glanced at my watch, my pace looked strong.

The real challenge wasn't in the water; it was getting out of it. The beach was made of loose, polished stones that shifted underfoot on a steep incline. Each step felt like climbing a landslide, but eventually I stumbled free, heart racing with accomplishment. I felt good about the swim. But my thoughts went straight back to the missing bike.

Still no sign of it when we returned to the hotel.

All day I carried the gnawing anxiety that I had come all this way only to be left without the gear I needed most.

Finally, at 9 p.m., the front desk called: My bike had arrived.

Relief washed over me as I carried the case upstairs, unboxed the bike, and carefully reassembled it. For the first time since landing, I could breathe a little easier. Yet one shadow still loomed large: the bike course itself.

Every athlete briefing, every article, every whispered conversation among competitors repeated the same phrase: *This is the hardest and most technical bike route on the IRONMAN circuit.*

That thought echoed in my mind as I joined the Parade of Nations later in the week. Around me were 2,500 athletes from 86 countries, flags waving, energy electric. The US was represented by 501 athletes, and I was one of 101 Legacy Athletes in the field. The rest were the fastest IRONMAN competitors on the planet. This was it. I belonged here. But I knew I was about to face the toughest test of my endurance yet.

Race Day

I slept surprisingly well the night before, and when my alarm went off at 4 a.m., I got right up. Breakfast was simple: two packs of oatmeal with peanut butter, mainly because we didn't have a kitchen in the room. We only had a coffee maker, with which I made hot water and put the oatmeal in a coffee cup, eating it by scooting the oatmeal out into my mouth with a coffee stirrer. I washed it down with an electrolyte drink and sipped slowly over the next hour.

My nerves weren't too bad because transition was literally across the street from our hotel. Convenience at its finest. At 5 a.m., I walked over to check on my bike, added my drink bottles, and made sure my tires were at the right pressure. Then I circled back to hand Andrea my morning clothes, zipped up my swim skin, and headed to the swim start.

This was it. It was really happening. Again.

The cannon fired for the pros, and one by one the age groups began moving toward the water. My age group didn't start until 45 minutes later, so I stood there watching, feeling the anticipation grow.

Finally, we waded out and treaded water for a couple of minutes, and then the horn sounded. I settled into my stroke quickly, locking into a steady rhythm. The entire swim I was surrounded by other athletes but avoided too many kicks and collisions.

After the first lap, I checked my watch and was making good time. Heading back out for lap two, I focused on conserving energy, knowing I would need every ounce for the bike. As the shore came into view, I picked up my pace slightly, exited the water, unzipped my suit, and jogged into transition.

Inside the tent, I fueled quickly, grabbed my helmet and bike shoes, and stuffed a peanut butter and jelly sandwich down my jersey. I rolled my bike out for what I knew would be the hardest IRONMAN ride of my life.

The bike started easily enough along the flat roads beside the Mediterranean. But after 30 minutes, we turned inland and hit a climb with gradients of 15 to 17 percent. My first thought: *If the whole course is like this, I may not finish.* Sweat poured down my face, and it was still early morning. That first climb was only the beginning. For nearly 60 miles, it was relentless: up, up, and more up.

At the special-needs station around mile 60, another exhausted athlete asked out loud, "Does it ever go downhill?"

A great question, not only for a bike course, but for life.

In the middle of hard seasons, we ask the same thing: *When will this get easier?*

I kept glancing at the cutoff times taped to my bike stem. I was about 30 minutes ahead, enough cushion to keep me moving. At the bike cutoff, a massive charter bus waited to scoop up athletes who couldn't go on. That was humbling. But I wasn't about to ride that bus.

Finally, around mile 82, the course tilted downward.

Relief.

Except the descents were brutal in their own way: hairpin turns, open roads, traffic, and cobblestones through tiny villages. I sat up, feathered my brakes, and still hit 35 mph. Later I heard the pros were bombing down at 50 to 60 mph. No, thank you. I wanted to make it back in one piece.

Nutrition became a challenge.

Back around mile 20, I had reached for my carb bottle, only to discover that it had bounced out somewhere on the cobblestones. Thankfully, I had practiced with the on-course drinks provided at IRONMAN races and could adjust. By mile 40, though, I stopped sweating, a dangerous sign. I quickly grabbed an electrolyte drink loaded with 1,000 mg of salt, and within minutes, my body reset and I began sweating again.

Eight hours after starting the bike portion, I finally rolled back into transition. It had been one of the toughest rides I had ever done. I prayed a lot during that ride. And I remembered something I had heard repeatedly in athlete briefings: *Don't stop. Just keep going.* I also knew I couldn't give up with so many people tracking me on the IRONMAN race app.

Craig Alexander, one of the greatest IRONMAN champions, had said, "Training is baking the cake. Race day is putting on the icing." That echoed in my mind as I laced up my running shoes, grabbed my hat and bib, and started the marathon.

At first, I felt surprisingly good. I ran steadily through the first half—13.1 miles—before the wall hit. My shoulders ached from the stress and tension of the bike. My legs burned. Dehydration set in. I wasn't hungry. I didn't want another sports drink. I just wanted to cross the finish line.

Andrea was there at every turnaround, cheering me on, giving me energy each time I saw her. With one lap to go, 3.1 miles, a simple 5K, I dug deep.

The finish line grew louder, the announcer's voice booming over the speakers as each athlete crossed.

Then I stepped onto the red carpet.

The crowd roared as if I was the only one out there.

The lights, the music, the energy, all funneled into that final moment.

And then I heard it:

"From Tampa, Florida, Jason Millsaps, you are an IRONMAN!"

Sixteen times now. And it never gets old.

Postrace Reflections

Standing there with the medal around my neck, I realized that this finish line felt different from Kona. Kona had been about proving I could do it, validating 12 years of work, overcoming surgeries, silencing doubts. Nice was about proving I still *loved* doing it. That endurance wasn't just about chasing medals, but about testing myself against new challenges, experiencing new places, continuing to grow.

The question "What's next?" still lingered, but now I knew the answer: *Whatever I choose.*

Maybe I would race again. Maybe I wouldn't.

Maybe I would focus on coaching and helping others chase their dreams.

Maybe I would find a new challenge entirely.

The point wasn't the racing. It was the growth.

The discipline. The refusal to quit. The faith that carried me through every setback.

Those lessons transcended triathlon. They applied to everything— marriage, parenting, ministry, leadership, life itself.

Transformation

I learned that ordinary people can accomplish extraordinary things not through talent, but through persistence. Through showing up daily even when progress feels invisible. Through choosing to start again after every setback. I think back to when I could barely swim a lap, when my first marathon nearly broke me. Now a marathon feels like a "cooldown." I'm not a superstar. I'm seriously an average guy who just refuses to stop showing up.

Running may not be my future, but that's okay. There are ultra-distance bike and swim events waiting. Bigger mountains to hike. New challenges to test my limits. The real joy is in the journey, the transformation that comes when you don't quit, even when the climb seems endless. Because in racing, as in life, the secret isn't speed, perfection, or strength. The secret is simple: Don't stop. Just keep going.

The finish line in Nice wasn't an ending. It was proof that the journey itself, the daily discipline, the small improvements, the stubborn refusal to quit, was the real victory all along. Great leaders know the same truth: Perseverance is more powerful than talent. Vision sets the goal. But resilience carries you to the finish line.

The Questions

What would change if you stopped seeing finish lines as destinations and started seeing them as waypoints?

How would your approach to challenges shift if you raced from confidence instead of desperation?

What mountain in your life needs climbing not because you have to, but because the challenge itself makes you better?

The real question isn't whether you can finish. It's whether you're willing to keep starting.

16

Run Your Race

*"Let us run with perseverance
the race marked out for us."*
—HEBREWS 12:1

The finish line doesn't mean the race is over. In fact, I have learned that every finish line is simply a new starting point. After overcoming addiction, recovering from two surgeries, enduring countless setbacks, and experiencing moments of celebration and failure, I can confidently say, endurance is not just about physical strength. It is a mindset. A heart attitude. Faith in motion.

My story began with a pounding headache, a can of Red Bull, and a bottle of Excedrin. It grew through the quiet miles before sunrise, through races I thought I would never finish, and through prayers I was not sure God would answer the way I hoped.

But through it all—addiction, transformation, injury, recovery, and those sacred finish lines in Kona and Nice, I was being shaped. Not just into an athlete, but into a man of deeper faith and steadier leadership. And now, it's your turn.

Your 140.6 Race

Your personal 140.6 probably isn't a triathlon race. Maybe it's forgiving someone who hurt you deeply. Breaking a habit that has controlled you for years. Restoring a broken relationship. Starting the business you've been dreaming about. Leaving a toxic situation. Going back to school. Getting out of debt. Running that first 5K. Finally having the hard conversation you've been avoiding.

Your race is unique. It is the journey set out for only you. And it is hard. But it is worth it.

The beauty of endurance is that it doesn't discriminate. It doesn't care about your starting point, your past failures, or how many times you've quit before. It only asks one thing: Are you willing to start?

Start Before You're Ready

I wasn't ready when I jumped in the pool and swam 37 yards. I wasn't ready when I registered for my first triathlon. I wasn't ready when Scott suggested a full IRONMAN race over a salad bar. If I'd waited until I felt ready, I would still be sitting on my couch, drinking energy drinks, and wondering what might have been. Ready is a myth. Ready is the excuse we use to avoid starting. The truth is, you'll never feel completely prepared for the hard things worth doing.

Diana Nyad didn't feel ready at 64 when she attempted to swim from Cuba to Florida. But after four failed attempts over the previous 35 years, she finally succeeded. When asked about her achievement, she said, "Never, ever give up. You're never too old to chase your dreams."

You don't have to be great to start. You just have to start. Walk around the block. Write down your goals. Join that group. Sign up for the thing you've been putting off. Have the conversation. Take the first step. Start now. Start small. But start.

Find Your People

Andrea believed in me when I doubted. Scott saw potential in me before I could see it in myself. Coach Elizabeth taught me how to fuel properly. My parents supported this crazy dream from the beginning. The boys grew up watching their dad refuse to quit. This wasn't my journey alone; it was ours.

Who are your people? Who believes in you even when you don't believe in yourself? Who will cheer for you at mile 20 when everything hurts and quitting looks appealing? You need those people. Find them. Invite them into your journey. Let them carry you when you can't carry yourself. And maybe you need to be that person for someone else. Maybe your story is not about what you accomplish, but about who you help along the way.

Leadership is not always about having all the answers. Sometimes it's about showing up, being honest about your struggles, and proving that ordinary people with uncommon persistence can accomplish exceptional things when they refuse to quit.

Embrace Setbacks

I've been through two major back surgeries. I've walked entire marathons. I've had races where it seemed like everything went wrong. I've come really close to missing cutoff times, which would have resulted in a DNF. I've questioned whether my body could handle one more mile. Those weren't failures; they were setbacks that became teachers. The first surgery taught me that "not yet" doesn't mean "never." The second taught me the fine line between perseverance and stubbornness. Slow races showed me that crossing the finish line matters more than how fast you get there. Delays reminded me that God's timing rarely matches my own. And Coach Scott's DNF proved that a single bad day doesn't define who you are.

Your setbacks are not proof that you should quit. They are proof that you are in the ring, actually trying something hard. The only people who never face setbacks are those who never attempt anything difficult. When you hit your wall, and you will, remember that walls are there to test how badly you want what is on the other side.

The Real Victory

I have 16 IRONMAN race medals, 13 IRONMAN 70.3 race medals, two World Championship finishes, and countless awards from smaller races. They are collecting dust on shelves and hanging from hooks in my office. The medals are not the point. The point is who I became in the process.

The discipline I developed. The faith I built. The marriage I strengthened through shared sacrifice. The example I set for my sons. The people I have coached who are now chasing their own impossible goals.

The real victory is not the medal; it's who you become in the struggle. That is what I want you to understand: Your finish line is not about external validation. It's about internal transformation. When you cross your finish line, whatever that looks like, you will not just have accomplished something. You will have become someone. Someone who doesn't quit. Someone who faces fear and moves forward anyway. Someone who knows that setbacks are not endings, just detours. Someone who understands that the journey matters more than the destination.

The Challenge

So here's my challenge to you. First, identify your race. What is the one thing you've been telling yourself you can't do? What dream have you been putting off? What conversation have you been avoiding? What goal seems too big, too hard, too far away? Name it. Write it down. Make it real.

The second thing to do is start today. How many times have we said, "I'll start Monday" or "I'll start January 1st"? Those dates sound motivating, but they're just excuses in disguise. Why not start right now? Not next month. Not when conditions are perfect. Today.

Take one step. Make one phone call. Write down one goal. Register for one race. Have one honest conversation. Small actions create momentum. Momentum creates change. Change creates transformation.

Third, find your team. Who needs to know about this goal? Who will support you? Whom will you invite into this journey? Don't try to do this alone. And maybe, just maybe, you need to be that person for someone else. Maybe someone is waiting for you to believe in them before they can believe in themselves.

Fourth, expect some setbacks. It's going to happen. I don't want to discourage you, but they are coming. Your "flat tire" moments. Your "bone-on-bone" diagnoses. Your delays and disappointments. They don't mean you're on the wrong path. They mean you are on a path worth traveling. Every setback is preparation for the comeback.

Fifth, keep showing up. On the days you don't feel like it. When progress is invisible. When everyone else seems faster, stronger, more qualified. Show up anyway. Consistency beats talent. Persistence beats perfection. Stubbornness, when pointed in the right direction, beats almost everything.

Lastly, run with faith. Believe that God is working even when you can't see it. Trust that the struggle has purpose. Know that you are being shaped into something stronger through the process. And if you've never considered faith, or if you've walked away from it, I would encourage you to explore what it means to run with God instead of running alone. There's freedom in not carrying everything by yourself.

The Real Race

Kona was the dream. Nice was the celebration. But life is the real race.

Every finish line I crossed taught me that the real victory is not the medal; it's who you become in the struggle. The Apostle Paul wrote, "Let us run with perseverance the race marked out for us" (Hebrews 12:1). That's not a verse for athletes. It's for all of us. Your 140.6 mile race might be a difficult marriage, a career setback, a health crisis, or a hidden addiction. Whatever your course looks like, you don't have to run it alone. With faith, perseverance, and the right perspective, you can finish strong.

Life is a marathon, not a sprint. There will be moments when you want to quit, seasons when the weight feels too heavy to carry. But the goal is to keep going. To keep looking ahead. To take one more step, one more pedal stroke, one more pull through the water. To never give up. To never back down. To keep pushing through, pressing on, and running your race with perseverance.

The Choice

Thirteen years ago, I could barely swim 37 yards. I was addicted to energy drinks. Overweight. Out of shape. Headed toward an early grave. But I made a choice. Not a perfect choice, just a choice to start. And that choice changed everything.

You have the same choice today. You can close this book and go back to the life you've always known. The comfortable patterns. The safe choices. The excuses that have kept you from attempting the hard things. Or you can close this book and take the first step toward something bigger.

The question is not whether you're qualified. The question is whether you're willing. Willing to start before you're ready. Willing to show up when it's hard. Willing to keep going when everyone else quits. Willing to believe that ordinary people can accomplish extraordinary things.

Your 37 Yards

I don't know what your 37 yards looks like. Maybe it's one lap in the pool. One conversation with your spouse. One application to the program you've been avoiding. One decision to finally get help for the addiction you've been hiding. But I know this: Your race is waiting. And you were made to run it. Not because you are special. Not because you have some unique talent the rest of us don't have. But because you refuse to quit. Because you keep showing up. Because you have faith that the struggle has purpose.

Today is a new day. The alarm has already gone off. The starting line is in front of you. The choice is yours. Don't wait any longer. Your race is waiting. And you were made to finish strong.

The Truth

Before you close this book, I want to leave you with this: The race is not against anyone else. It is against the voice that says you can't. Against the fear that says you are not enough. Against the past that says you already failed. The race is between who you are and who you could become. And here is the beautiful truth about all of this: The finish line is not fixed. It keeps moving. Because growth does not end. Transformation does not stop. The journey does not conclude just because you crossed one finish line. There's always another mountain. Another challenge. Another opportunity to prove that you are stronger than you thought.

So run your race. Not mine. Not someone else's. Yours. The one that terrifies you. The one that makes you wonder if you can actually do it. The one that will require everything you have and then some. That race. Run it with everything you have. And when you cross the finish line, and you will, remember that it was never about the medal. It was about becoming the kind of person who refuses to quit. Now close this book. And start running.

THE END

DISCUSSION QUESTIONS FOR GROUPS

This book is designed to spark conversations about perseverance, faith, setbacks, and finishing strong. Whether you're reading with a church small group, book club, coaching group, or accountability partner, these questions will help you apply the principles to your own journey.

PART I: THE STARTING LINE (CHAPTERS 1–7)

CHAPTERS 1–2: WAKE-UP CALLS AND NEW BEGINNINGS

1. Jason's wake-up call involved seeing himself in a church video. What external mirror (a photo, comment, health scare, relationship) has forced you to confront uncomfortable truth?

2. Jason replaced energy drinks and Excedrin with healthier habits. What unhealthy coping mechanism do you need to replace? What would you replace it with?

3. Jason's marathon disaster taught him that "attempting big things without proper preparation doesn't make you brave—it makes you reckless." When have you confused boldness with foolishness? What did you learn?

4. What's the difference between a finish line that changes you and one that just gives you a medal?

CHAPTER 3: 37 YARDS AND FINDING A GUIDE

1. Jason could swim only 37 yards on his first attempt. What's your "37 yards"—something you tried that humbled you immediately?

2. Scott saw potential in Jason before Jason could see it in himself. Who has been your "Scott"? How did they change your trajectory?

3. Are you currently someone's Scott—believing in them before they believe in themselves? If not, who needs you to step into that role?

4. Jason met with Scott "over a salad bar." Sometimes the most important conversations happen in ordinary places. What seemingly small encounter changed your life?

CHAPTERS 4–7: BUILDING THE FOUNDATION

1. Training for Jason's first IRONMAN race meant 4:30 a.m. alarms and sacrificing family time. How do you balance pursuing personal goals with responsibilities to others?

2. Andrea supported Jason's training even when it was inconvenient. How do you support the people you love in their goals, even when it costs you something?

3. Jason learned that "progress rarely comes suddenly. It comes from showing up daily, trusting the process, refusing to quit when it gets hard." What daily habits or practices are you building that will sustain you through future challenges?

4. Jason's faith carried him "when strength ran out." When has your faith (in God, in the process, in yourself) been tested? How did it sustain you?

PART II: THE MIDDLE MILES (CHAPTERS 8–11)

CHAPTERS 8–9: WHEN RACES (AND BODIES) BREAK YOU

1. Louisville and Texas taught Jason that "sometimes survival is success." When have you had to redefine success because circumstances made your original goal impossible?

2. Coach Scott, with nine IRONMAN race finishes, didn't make the cutoff in Texas. What does this teach you about the relationship between experience and outcomes?

3. Jason's body eventually broke after 12 IRONMAN races. How do you know when pushing through becomes destructive rather than productive?

4. After his first surgery, Jason said, "Sometimes the body says no, and you have to listen. But 'no' doesn't always mean 'never.' Sometimes it just means 'not yet.'" How does this perspective change how you view setbacks?

5. Lying on the garage floor unable to move, Jason faced the possibility that his racing career was over. What identity have you had to release? How did you discover who you were without it?

CHAPTERS 10–11: STUBBORNNESS VS. PERSEVERANCE

1. Jason raced IRONMAN Tulsa knowing his disc was destroyed and surgery was scheduled the following week. Was this courage or foolishness? Where's the line?

2. He asks, "How do you know when perseverance becomes stubbornness?" How would you answer this question in your own context (career, relationship, goal)?

3. What example are you setting for people watching your life? Would they learn healthy perseverance or destructive stubbornness?

4. During recovery, Jason obtained coaching certifications, transforming waiting time into preparation time. What could you be preparing for while you wait?

5. Jason deferred his Kona dream twice. When has a delay ultimately worked in your favor, even though it felt like failure at the time?

PART III: THE FINISH LINE (CHAPTERS 12–16)

CHAPTERS 12–13: RACE WEEK AND THE RACE OF A LIFETIME

1. Jason stood on the Kona starting line 12 years after barely swimming 37 yards. What "impossible" goal are you 1, 5, or 10 years away from achieving if you refuse to quit?

2. Jason realized Kona was "the culmination of both our sacrifices," recognizing Andrea's role in his achievement. What would your "Kona" be? What's the goal that would represent not just your effort, but also the support of those who helped you get there?

3. Jason's family sacrificed to support his dream. Who has sacrificed to support you? Have you acknowledged their role in your achievements?

4. At the end of Chapter 13, Jason reflects that "the finish line isn't the reward—it's proof that you never quit. The real victory is who you become in the struggle." How has your journey changed who you are, regardless of whether you've reached your finish line yet?

CHAPTER 14: THE SPACE BETWEEN

1. Jason describes post-Kona emptiness: "Now what?" Have you experienced this after achieving a long-pursued goal? How did you navigate it?

2. He references Moses (40 years in the desert) and Joseph (years in prison) as examples of God working in "the space between." What season of waiting or uncertainty are you in right now? How might God be forming you through it?

3. Jason started coaching, passing forward what Scott had given him. What do you need to pass forward? Who needs what you've learned?

CHAPTERS 15–16: NICE AND RUNNING YOUR RACE

1. Jason raced Nice "from joy, not desperation." How would your life change if your motivation shifted from proving something to celebrating something?

2. He writes, "The race isn't the destination. The race is part of the journey." What would change if you saw your current challenge as part of a longer story rather than the whole story?

3. Jason's "37 yards" became coaching others toward their finish lines. How has your greatest struggle positioned you to help others?

4. Your 140.6 probably isn't a triathlon race. What is your 140.6? What's the seemingly impossible thing you need to attempt?

CLOSING REFLECTION

1. Jason concludes, "You don't have to be great to start. You just have to start." What have you been waiting to feel "ready" for? What would starting today look like?

2. Jason's story is organized around the Starting Line, the Middle Miles, and the Finish Line. Which section are you in right now? What do you need to do to keep moving forward?

3. What's your "37 yards"—the first small step you'll take this week toward your impossible goal?

4. Jason writes, "The finish line doesn't mean the race is over. . . . Every finish line is simply a new starting point." What finish line have you crossed that was actually a new beginning?

5. On a scale of 1 to 10, how would you rate your current level of perseverance? What would move you one number higher?

6. Jason's core message is: "Ordinary people can accomplish extraordinary things when they refuse to quit." What extraordinary thing is waiting for you on the other side of not quitting?

FOR GROUP LEADERS

These questions are designed to be used flexibly.

- 4-Week Study: Focus on 9 to 10 questions per week, organized by book parts.
- 8-Week Study: Cover two or three chapters per week with 5 or 6 questions per session.
- 16-Week Deep Dive: Work on one chapter per week with 3 or 4 focused questions.
- One-Day Retreat: Select 15 to 20 questions that resonate most with your group's season. Encourage participants to: (1) Read chapters before discussion. (2) Journal responses to questions privately first. (3) Share honestly about struggles, not just successes. (4) Commit to one action step per discussion. (5) Follow up with accountability partners between sessions.

For additional resources or training plans,
or to book Jason for your group or event:

www.121TriCoaching.com

APPENDIX:
COMPLETE RACE HISTORY

SPRINT TRIATHLONS

2012

▫ Las Campanas Sprint Triathlon—Santa Fe, New Mexico

2013

▫ John Tanner Sprint Triathlon—Carrollton, Georgia

5K TO 10K RACES

2012

▫ Rio Rancho 5K—Rio Rancho, New Mexico
▫ Thanksgiving Day 8K Turkey Trot—Knoxville, Tennessee

2013

▫ Peachtree Road Race 10K—Atlanta, Georgia
▫ Thanksgiving Day Hot to Trot 5K—Knoxville, Tennessee

2014

▫ Club Chase 5K—Athens, Georgia
▫ Habitat Hustle 5K—Watkinsville, Georgia

2015

▫ Gasparilla 5K—Tampa, Florida
▫ Thanksgiving Day Hot to Trot 5K—Knoxville, Tennessee

2024

▫ Thanksgiving Day Turkey Gobble 5K—Tampa, Florida

IRONMAN 70.3® / HALF-DISTANCE TRIATHLON RACES

2013

▫ IRONMAN 70.3 Florida—Haines City, Florida

2014

▫ Rev 3 Half-Distance Triathlon—Knoxville, Tennessee
▫ Rock 'n' Roll Georgia Half-Distance Triathlon—Georgia

2015

▫ Hits Half-Distance Triathlon—Ocala, Florida

2016

▫ Hits Half-Distance Triathlon—Naples, Florida
▫ Florida Challenge Half-Distance Triathlon—Clermont, Florida
▫ IRONMAN 70.3 Gulf Coast—Panama City Beach, Florida
▫ IRONMAN 70.3 Augusta—Augusta, Georgia

2017

▫ Hits Half-Distance Triathlon—Naples, Florida
▫ IRONMAN 70.3 Florida—Haines City, Florida

2020

▫ Clash Half-Distance Triathlon—Daytona International Speedway, Florida

2021

▫ Clash Half-Distance Triathlon—Daytona International Speedway, Florida

2024

□ IRONMAN 70.3 Gulf Coast—Panama City Beach, Florida

IRONMAN® 140.6 RACES

2013

□ IRONMAN Arizona—Tempe, Arizona (13:54:15)

2014

□ IRONMAN Louisville—Louisville, Kentucky (14:42:41)

2015

□ IRONMAN Texas—The Woodlands, Texas (16:28:30)

2016

□ IRONMAN Florida—Panama City Beach, Florida (13:48:45)

2017

□ IRONMAN Florida—Panama City Beach, Florida (13:53:24)

2018

□ IRONMAN Texas—The Woodlands, Texas (13:12:37)
□ IRONMAN Chattanooga*—Chattanooga, Tennessee (12:09:03)
Swim canceled due to conditions.
□ IRONMAN Florida—Haines City, Florida (14:01:47)

2019

□ IRONMAN Texas—The Woodlands, Texas (13:52:30)
□ IRONMAN Florida—Haines City, Florida (14:05:15)

2021

□ IRONMAN Lake Placid—Lake Placid, New York (15:03:26)
□ IRONMAN Arizona—Tempe, Arizona (14:09:18)

2022

□ IRONMAN Waco—Waco, Texas (16:12:10)

2023

□ IRONMAN Tulsa—Tulsa, Oklahoma (13:52:02)

2024

□ IRONMAN World Championship—Kona, Hawaii (13:58:34)

2025

□ IRONMAN World Championship—Nice, France (15:28:45)

SPECIAL ACHIEVEMENTS

□ Solo Ride Across Florida (2015)
150 miles (9:59:35)
Siesta Key Beach to Fort Pierce

□ Open-Water Swim
Lake Lanier 5K Swim Race—Gainesville, Georgia (2014)

□ Legacy Program
Accepted into IRONMAN Legacy Program (2022)
Completed IRONMAN World Championship in
Kona, Hawaii 2024
Completed IRONMAN World Championship in
Nice, France (2025)

Total Career Statistics

□ IRONMAN 140.6 Races: 16

□ IRONMAN 70.3 / Half-Distance Triathlon Races: 13

□ Sprint Triathlons: 2

□ Various 5K, 8K, and 10K Races

COACHING CREDENTIALS

- USAT (USA Triathlon) Level 1 Certified Coach—Long Distance Focus
- TrainingPeaks Level 2 Certified Coach
- Founder, 121 Tri Coaching, LLC

REFERENCES AND RECOMMENDED READING

BOOKS REFERENCED

Clear, James. *Atomic Habits: An Easy* and *Proven Way to Build Good Habits and Break Bad Ones*. New York: Avery, 2018.

Duckworth, Angela. *Grit: The Power of Passion and Perseverance*. New York: Scribner, 2016.

Kouzes, James M., and Barry Z. Posner. *The Leadership Challenge: How to Make Extraordinary Things Happen in Organizations*. 6th ed. Hoboken, NJ: Wiley, 2017.

Maxwell, John C. *The 15 Invaluable Laws of Growth: Live Them and Reach Your Potential*. New York: Center Street, 2012.

Maxwell, John C. *Sometimes You Win, Sometimes You Learn: Life's Greatest Lessons Are Gained from Our Losses*. New York: Center Street, 2013.

Maxwell, John C. *The 21 Irrefutable Laws of Leadership: Follow Them and People Will Follow You*. Nashville: Thomas Nelson, 2007.

Nyad, Diana. *Find a Way: One Wild and Precious Life*. New York: Knopf, 2015.

Rice, Helen Steiner. "The Bend in the Road." Poem concept referenced with attribution. Fleming H. Revell Company, 1965.

Sinek, Simon. *The Infinite Game*. New York: Portfolio/Penguin, 2019.

SCRIPTURE REFERENCES

All scripture quotations are taken from the Holy Bible, New International Version®, NIV®. Copyright © 1973, 1978, 1984, 2011 by Biblica, Inc.™ Used by permission of Zondervan. All rights reserved worldwide.

COACHING AND PROFESSIONAL RESOURCES

Bennefield, Scott. USAT Certified Level 2 Triathlon Coach, NASM Certified Personal Trainer, nine-time IRONMAN finisher, three-time cancer survivor, Personal coaching engagement, 2012–2024. Founder: Para Endurance Coaching & Para Endurance Foundation www.paraendurance.com, scott@paraendurance.com

Inpyn, Elizabeth. Sports nutritionist and performance coach. Personal coaching and nutritional consultation, 2023–2025.

USA Triathlon (USAT). Level 1 Coaching Certification Program—Long Distance Focus. Completed 2023.

TrainingPeaks. Level 2 Coaching Certification Program. Completed 2023.

MEDICAL PROFESSIONALS

Fromke, Michael, MD, MBA. Neurosurgeon, Fort Myers, Florida. Surgical care and medical consultation, 2022–2024.

INSPIRATIONAL QUOTES

Quotations from public figures including Zig Ziglar, Nelson Mandela, Tommy Lasorda, T. S. Eliot, Robert Collier, Babe Ruth, Walter Elliot, William Feather, C. S. Lewis, and Mike Tyson have been attributed as accurately as possible. Some quotes have become part of common motivational vernacular, and original attribution may be disputed.

Alexander, Craig. Three-time IRONMAN World Champion. Quote: "Training is baking the cake. Race day is putting on the icing."

ADDITIONAL RESOURCES

American Society of Addiction Medicine. "Definition of Addiction." 2019. https://www.asam.org/quality-care/definition-of-addiction

IRONMAN®. Official race information and athlete resources. https://www.ironman.com

TrainingPeaks. Endurance training platform and education. https://www.trainingpeaks.com

USA Triathlon. Official training and coaching resources. https://www.usatriathlon.org

ABOUT COUCH TO 5K

The Couch to 5K (C25K) program referenced in this book is a popular running plan designed to take beginners from sedentary to running a 5K (3.1 miles) in nine weeks. Various versions exist, but the program mentioned follows the basic interval training structure of alternating walking and running, gradually increasing running duration over time.

FOR MORE INFORMATION

For coaching inquiries or to learn more about the author's journey:

121 Tri Coaching: www.121TriCoaching.com

ABOUT THE AUTHOR

JASON MILLSAPS is a worship pastor, endurance athlete, and certified triathlon coach based in Tampa, Florida. Since December 2014, Jason has served as the lead worship pastor at Bell Shoals Church, a multi-campus church in west-central Florida.

Jason became a Christ follower at age 6 and surrendered to full-time ministry at 17. He holds a bachelor's degree in music with an emphasis/minor in business administration from Carson Newman University, a master's degree in worship from Southwestern Baptist Theological Seminary, and a graduate certificate in management and leadership from Liberty University. He has served churches in Texas, Georgia, New Mexico, and Florida.

Jason's journey into endurance sports began in August 2012 when he could barely swim 37 yards without stopping. Over 13 years, he completed 16 IRONMAN races (140.6 miles), including two World Championships—Kona, Hawaii (2024) and Nice, France (2025). He has also completed 13 IRONMAN 70.3 and half-distance triathlon races, 2 sprint triathlons, and numerous 5K, 8K, and 10K road races.

Despite facing two major spinal surgeries (microdiscectomy in 2022, spinal fusion in 2023) that threatened to end his racing career, Jason persevered through extensive rehabilitation and returned to competition. His story demonstrates that ordinary people can accomplish extraordinary things through faith, persistence, and refusing to quit.

Following his racing achievements and recovery experiences, Jason became a certified triathlon coach through USA Triathlon (USAT Level 1, Long Distance focus) and TrainingPeaks (Level 2). In 2023 he founded 121 Tri Coaching, LLC, through which he helps athletes of all levels pursue their own endurance goals. His coaching philosophy emphasizes sustainable training, proper nutrition, and mental resilience.

Jason lives in Tampa, Florida, with his wife Andrea and their two sons, Jonathan and Jaden. When he's not leading worship or coaching athletes, you might find Jason swimming, biking, or running (more like walking) the roads of west-central Florida—though these days he's more likely to be helping someone else chase their finish line than chasing his own.

CONNECT WITH JASON

Triathlon coaching: 121 Tri Coaching, LLC
www.121TriCoaching.com

Offering:

- Personalized training plans for all distances—sprint, Olympic, IRONMAN 70.3, and IRONMAN
- One-on-one coaching with weekly check-ins
- Nutrition guidance and race-day strategy
- Beginner-friendly programs (specialty: athletes starting from "37 yards")

Speaking Engagements:

Jason is available to speak at:
- Churches and faith-based conferences
- Corporate wellness events and leadership retreats
- Endurance sports clubs and triathlon expos
- Men's ministry gatherings
- Motivational events focused on perseverance, overcoming setbacks, and finishing strong

Contact for speaking inquiries: jemillsaps@gmail.com
Bulk Book Orders:
Discounts available for:
- Church small groups and book studies
- Corporate gifts and wellness program resources
- Endurance sports clubs and teams
- Coaching groups and training groups

For orders of 10 or more copies, email: jemillsaps@gmail.com

Stay Connected:

Instagram: @121tricoaching, @jemillsaps

A WORD FROM JASON

This book isn't just my story, it's a mirror. If an out-of-shape worship pastor addicted to energy drinks can swim 2.4 miles, bike 112 miles, and run a marathon in one day after two back surgeries, what's possible for you?

Your "37 yards" might be one conversation you've been avoiding, one habit you need to break, one dream you've been dismissing as impossible. But I've learned that transformation doesn't require talent. It requires showing up—especially on the days when you don't feel like it.

I'm still running my race. Still showing up at 4:30 a.m. Still learning that every finish line is just a new starting point.

The question isn't whether you're qualified. The question is: Are you willing to start?

Your race is waiting. Let's run it together.

— Jason Millsaps
Tampa, Florida

Made in the USA
Columbia, SC
20 January 2026

77819855R00125